HOW TO KEEP YOUR WARDROBE UPDATED

Written and Illustrated

By

MARIE WOODRUFF © 2016

ISBN: 1501046888
ISBN 13:9781501046889

Library of Congress Control Number: 2016911531
CreateSpace Independent Publishing Platform, North Charleston, SC

HOW TO KEEP YOUR WARDROBE UPDATED

SCOPE OF THE WORK:

Part I - By selectively collecting clothes, keeping in mind classic styling, natural fabrics, and versatility, and adding to your wardrobe from season to season, rather than replacing it, you can amass a fortune in a beautiful wardrobe and stay fashionably in style year after year.

Part II - By minimal upgrading, redesigning, and repairing of, and perpetual extending to, your wardrobe, your clothes can withstand both the ravages of wear and tear and the "fad" fashions.

PREFACE

Until twenty-five years ago, the so-called international socialites spent most of their time for fittings with their couturiers, playing, and partying, and all the other paraphenalia that went with this narcissistic set. During the Victorian Era there unabashedly existed socialities with the title "Professional Beauty." Their letters were P.B. Most of today's real women are too busy, and enlightened, to be caught up in a maze of uninvolvement beyond the self that leads to nothing more than a dead living corpse. Even today's richest women find it much more exciting, and practical, to be providing for a home for their family, or pursuing a career, or building a financial empire, rather than building an entirely new designer or couture wardrobe every season year after year. With today's myriad of social, political, and economical woes, women need to learn how to shop wisely for clothes as an investment. The short term, throw-away, disposable era is totally unpractical, unnecessary, and unmodern. Furthermore, today's woman rarely has the time to follow fashion fads and trends, or even to shop; therefore, she will probably want to add only a few new, fine quality items, mostly accessories, to her existing wardrobe, just as she would to her collection of fine porcelains. Or she may want to use the clothes she has and redesign them in order to stay in current fashion. Or she may not economically be able to have a wardrobe of her choice and will have to improvise by both buying basic clothes and learning how to redesign and coordinate her clothes. Above all, clothes should be fun, not a seasonal financial burden. And you need not be a great seamstress to learn how to redesign a few items here and there. If you have a semester or two of high school sewing, you will not have trouble following my simple suggestions on how to update your clothes.

Women today are on the move: they need clothes they can move in; they also need clothes that will move with them. Gone are the elaborate Marie Antoinette days when women existed solely for the man, without an identity of their own and spent all their time on themselves--for their man. During the nineteenth century so elaborate and ornate were women's clothes that women were merely props for the purpose of displaying their clothes to the public or whomever they were trying to impress. And gone are the days when women endured pain for the sake of fashion, when neck collars were large enough to encircle a horse, and skirts were wide enough to sweep the grand ballroom of the Tajh Mahal. And more recently, pencil skirts of the fifties and early sixties were so narrow that women could take only a few short steps at a time. Can you see today's busy executive in that type of attire?

The mini skirts of the late sixties contributed to the revolution of women's philosophy about their clothing. The elder ladies refused to accept the mini skirt. The younger set did, but when fashion designers attempted to drastically lower the hemlines, they met with resistence. Hot pants were a compromise, but it was too late. Women had had enough. They were becoming liberated and began to wear whatever they pleased. Today women are liberated, and anything goes anywhere. As a result, skirts and pants of all lengths and widths are "in." Jeans may be worn for gardening as well as for dinner dates. With careful shopping of clothes in fine fabrics and simple lines, and with proper care, whatever you buy can remain forever in your style. Have you ever noticed how some of the most successful women create their own fashions? And there is a growing trend in fashion today to wear "international" clothes. Examples of this are the American western attire, the Russian Cossack pants, the Chinese mandarin jacket, the Bermuda and Jamaica shorts, the English nautical look, the African Safari jacket, and so on. Most of these are classic items that can be worn for many, many years in their original styles, or they can be slightly redesigned for a new look. Others can be collector's items for hostess party clothes or for costume parties. With such a liberated outlook on women's fashions, it is wise, therefore, to buy your clothes with investment for the future in mind.

INTRODUCTION

Fashion reflects the times: social, political, and economic.

Throughout fashion history, women's fashions changed very little from year to year, except for the latter part of the eighteenth century, when the French Revolution brought a sudden halt to extravagantly glamorous and ostentatious women's clothing that would never return for everyday wear. During the nineteenth century, with rapidly progressive social and technical advances, fashion change became more frequent, with each fashion period lasting from five to ten years. Today, with social, political and economic philosophies and technologies orbiting at an accelerated rate, fashion changes yearly, even seasonally. If today's woman wants to stay "in style," she must pay the price. This book, therefore, reflects the economic times that have emanated from our years of social and political problems and the need to economize, even in fashion.

From the beginning of time, and encompassing all times, fashion has been basic in line, style, fabric, and color. The scope of this book is to show the fashion-conscious woman how to start with and work on the basics and the classics, and how to build and update, rather than replace, her wardrobe from year to year. This book is not for the international best-dressed status seeker; it is for the woman who is unable to or does not care to spend a great deal of money on her wardrobe, but does want to dress fashionably.

I have frequently noted that the best dressed woman is invariably the one who is likely to say," I've had this for years," about most of her clothes. Like the astute investor who buys quality arts and antiques for both aesthetic and investment purposes, the smart woman <u>invests</u> in quality basic and classic clothes as a foundation to her wardrobe, and merely adds new pieces or redefines her old ones to update the total look. In these uncertain times when money is tight and precious, it is economically unwise for today's woman to spend a small fortune on a completely new wardrobe every season, regardless of her socioeconomic situation.

Marie Woodruff

San Diego, California

TABLE OF CONTENTS

HOW TO KEEP YOUR WARDROBE UPDATED

PART I

LET'S GO BACK TO THE BASICS

Chapter I

The 12-Point Guide to Selecting Your Basic Clothes

Not every woman will fit into the basic wardrobe category. The woman who is an outdoor casual type in California is going to have different needs from the sophisticated Studio 54 type in New York; the established oil tycoon from Houston will differ from the shifty politician in Washington; and the traditional homemaker in arrid Utah will not dress like the liberated career woman in humid Hawaii.

I consider pants and skirts as the foundation to your wardrobe, and beige in all its different tones, blacks, and the whites as the most basic and versatile neutral colors. Use your pants and skirts as a backdrop for your tops, sweaters, and jackets. As designer Liz Claiborne said, "Keep your pants and skirts neutral. Get variety in your tops" (Vogue, November 1980).

Because every woman's needs are unique, I have developed The 12-Point Guide to Selecting Your Basic Clothes (Fig. I-1). Each point is fully discussed and should aid most women who are interested in getting the most value out of their clothing investment any place in the world.

1. Is it seasonless?

In today's tight economy there is a strong emphasis on clothes that are seasonless. Not only do women want their clothes to work for them year-after-year, their clothes must also work year-round.

Fashion designer Geoffrey Beene said that half of a woman's wardrobe should be seasonless to include a weightless raincoat; a silk cardigan to wear as a blouse or sweater; sweaters in cotton, silk, or rayon; pants in corduroy and silk. Anne Klein feels that a woman's wardrobe should be about thirty percent seasonless to be achieved through seasonless fabrics: leathers and suedes, silks, cashmere, fine flannel, and all types of wools and cottons (Vogue, January 1981).

I live at the coast in California where the weather is moderately even throughout the year; therefore, most of my clothes are seasonless. However, a woman living in Canada where there are distinctive seasons would have a more difficult time choosing seasonless clothing. A leather pants coat might be her choice for a seasonless coat, especially one with a zip-out lining.

2.   Is it classic in design?

A classic design is one that remains in style year-after-year. A classic is a simple, basic design from which all fads and trendy clothes come and go. Fashion cycles always go back to the classics. Classics are the foundation of a good basic wardrobe.

Avoid fussy, frilly, cute clothes. The key word to remember is understatement. It is better to be underdressed than overdressed. American designer Galanos, talking about his secret of good design, says that he does not like pretty, sweet, overdone clothes. If he uses a ruffle, it is used as a point in design, not just something to tack on.

The straight leg pants, about 18" around the bottom, are a classic design from which came the bell bottoms, lounging and hostess pyjamas, bloomers, balloons, palazzos, knickbockers, capris, gauchos, clam diggers, pedal pushers, knickers, cossacks, culottes, walking shorts, bermudas, jamaicas, rehearsal shorts, hot pants, short shorts, hip huggers, jeans, overalls, jumpsuits, stretch pants, jodhpurs...just to mention a few of the most commonly known pants in recent years of fashion. Within this range, however, are also classics because they are basic and work year-after-year: culottes, bermudas, western style jeans, riding jodhpurs, stretch ski pants, athletic short shorts, and hostess pyjamas. In addition to the straight leg pants, almost every item of clothing is available in the classic cut: the simple black dress, the jumper, the shirt blouse, the V-neck cardigan, the A-line skirt, the trench coat, the prep blazer, the basic pump, the swagger handbag. If you own only one of each of these pieces in your favorite basic color, in a fine quality natural or natural-blend fabric, you would need to add only the occasional piece, again basic, to create virtually an infinite variety of outfits and stay in style for several years.

The more simple the garment, the more diversely you can accessorize it. If you own a good basic dress in a basic color and ruffles are a hot item you cannot resist that season, work some ready-made ruffles or your own created ruffles into the design of the basic dress either in the same or contrasting color and fabric of the dress. When ruffles are out of style, remove the ruffles from the basic dress and work with other accessories, such as sweaters, jackets, jewelry, and scarves.

Try to think of your clothes as a fine, long-term investment. It is better to own one fine-quality classic shirt blouse in white silk or cotton than ten flashy cheapies that will go out of style in a season. Many turn-of-the-century styles, such as boleros, capes, fringed shawls, knickers, dirndle skirts, shirt blouses, V-neck cardigans, and country blazers are only a few of the classics that could be still worn today.

3. <u>Is it timeless in fabric?</u>

Good basic clothes are made of the best quality fabrics, which include natural fibers or natural-blend fibers. The world's foremost designers work almost exclusively in natural, so-called luxury fibers: wool, silk, cotton, and linen, as well as the skins: furs and leather. Rayon and celanese are man-made fibers made from natural products.

Natural fibers are of animal or plant origin: wool and specialty wools come from the hair and fur of animals, such as the sheep, cashmere and angora goats, camel, alpaca, llama, and vicuna; cotton from the seed of the cotton boll; silk from the secretion of the silkworm; and linen from the stalk of the flax plant. The skins come from almost any animal, including the reptiles, that are not on the endangered species list.

Even though many natural fibers have been replaced by or supplemented with synthetic fibers, the natural fibers are prestigious and expensive today because they stand up well against time and wear. Almost ironically, although understandably, during these difficult economic times women are buying better quality but fewer garments in the natural fibers (and classic lines) that are expensive initially, but more economical as a long-term investment.

(a) <u>Wool</u> - Pure wool is symbolized by the Pure Wool insignia established by the International Wool Secretariat Woolmark. Wool has been used for clothing for 6,000 years, and is referenced in the Bible.

The main sheep raising countries are Australia, New Zealand, South Africa, South America, and the British Isles. Merino sheep from Australia produce the finest wool.

Wool is desirable because it is made up of small sections that enable the fibers flexibility and durability, giving wool fiber a special springy, resilient quality that cannot be imitated by man-made fibers. Wool is also a superior fiber because it can absorb 40% of its weight without feeling damp; it is flame-proof and acts as a natural insulator by keeping body heat close to the body; it can be shaped by heat and moisture.

Cashmere and angora rabbit fibers are among the softest and most expensive of the wools. Sheep wool fibers are the most popular, made in a wide range of textures and textiles. Some woolcloths, such as beaver cloth, doeskin, sealskin, and sharkskin are made to imitate the skins, but are in fact wools. Others are blends of the natural or the man-made fibers. Tropical cloths and viyella are examples of blends, although almost all wools can be blended with other fibers. See Appendix I for the different types of wool.

(b) Silk - Silk is a continuous filament of protein substances that comes from the cocoon of a silkworm which feeds from the leaf of the mulberry tree. Some other species of silkworm produce a course silk and feed on the leaves of the oak, castor oil, and cherry trees. Silk production dates to 2640 B. C. in China. Henry Barham wrote in 'An

Essay Upon the Silkwork' (London, 1719) that silkworms survived the Great Flood and in time made their way to China by Noah.

Silk is synonymous with expensive and designer clothes. Silk has some unique characteristics not found in other fabrics: it has a luxurious look and hand with a natural, soft luster, lively suppleness, and excellent draping qualities. Chiffon is the finest of all silks; raw silk is the most durable.

Unlike the other natural fibers, silk does not breathe, therefore, creates a perspiration problem to some of those who wear it in warm weather because of its tight weave and low moisture absorbency.

See Appendix II for the different types of silk.

(c) <u>Cotton</u> - Cotton is a fluffy vegetable fiber (cotton boll) which grows from the seed pod of the cotton plant. Cotton has been used in making clothing for 3,500 years, having begun in India. Historical writings are replete with evidence that cotton was used in the times of ancient Rome, Greece, Egypt, Peru, Persia (Iran), China, and Japan.

In 1607 cotton was grown in North America for commercial use. In 1793 Eli Whitney, an American, invented the cotton gin which separated the cotton fiber from the seeds, and America became the largest producer of cotton in the world.

The characteristics of the quality of cotton fiber include its staple length (1/2 to 2 inches), crimpness (natural ribbon-like twists of the fiber), fineness, uniformity and maturity of the fibers, color, and cleanliness. Because each cotton fiber is tubular in structure, cotton garments breathe, which means that they absorb and release moisture rapidly, thereby making cotton comfortable for hot weather wear. Cotton is also durable and inexpensive.

Leading designers of women's clothing prefer 100% cotton when using this fabric. Cotton has a wide range of textures--from the sheer dotted Swiss muslins to the rugged corduroys. According to Cotton Incorporated of America, the preferred quality of cotton is the cotton/polyester blend, with the cotton content being 60 to 70%. The cotton/polyester fabrics have all the advantages of cotton, plus they are virtually wrinkle-free, making them a highly ideal fabric for today's busy people in a tight economy. However, sunlight oxidizes cotton, which causes the whites and pastels to yellow, and all cottons to deteriorate with age.

Denim is the most versatile and widely utilized of all the cottons, being used for both blue collar working clothes and designer jeans.

See Appendix III for the different types of cottons.

(d) Linen - Linen is made from the stalk of flax. The history of linen is recorded in hieroglyphics dating back 7,000 years when the Egyptians gathered flax along the banks of the Nile and made it into products from rope and fishing items to clothing and mummy wrappings. Ireland is the most famous for its linen industry, although Russia is the largest producer of flax.

Flax is the strongest of all vegetable fibers and is almost 100% cellulose in its processed state. Special properties of linen are its attractive texture of thick and thin yarns; its durability due to its strong fibers; its comfort because it is a good conductor of heat. The disadvantage of linen is that it has low flexibility, therefore, it wrinkles easily. However, many garments today are treated with wrinkle-free finishes.

Like wool and silk, linen is a prestigious and expensive fabric because of its limited production. It is a favorite choice for fine-quality clothing, particularly suits and tailored-look dresses.

(e) <u>Man-made Fabrics</u> - Scarcity and the high cost of silk led to the man-made fiber industry. Being a continuous solid fiber, silk was easy to synthesize.

Count Hilaire de Chardonnet, a French inventor, made the first successful chemical fiber from cellulose in 1884. Edwin J. Beer, a British inventor, developed the process of viscose rayon. By 1913, Britain was producing over 3 million pounds of "artificial silk." In 1909 Samuel Courtauld, a British company, bought the rights to produce viscose rayon, then known as "artificial silk," which was first produced in the U.S.A. in 1910. Acetate was produced in America in 1925. Both rayon and acetate are man-made fibers produced from natural sources.

In 1938 nylon was developed by DuPont de Nemours. Nylon is

strong, elastic, mothproof, moisture resistant, and rot-resistant. In 1941 polyester was invented in Britain; by 1953 Du Pont began producing polyester under the name of Dacron. In 1962 Du Pont introduced polyurethane known as Spandex for making elasticated fibers.

The two basic types of man-made fibers are:

(a) Regenerated cellulose: rayon and acetate made from the natural cellulose of pine trees or cotton linters.

(b) Synthetic polymer: acrylic, polyester, nylon, polyethylene, polypropylene, polyurethane, and polyvinylchloride.

Man-made fibers are made by pumping plastic liquid through tiny holes of a nozzle, jet, or spinneret. As the streams of plastic material solidify by coagulation, evaporation, or cooling, they become continuous filaments of thread, in imitation of the method the silkworm uses to produce its continuous filaments of silk. Nylon and polyester are the most popular man-made fibers.

Some of the main properties of man-made fibers are that they are primarily inexpensive and crease-resistant, as well as soft, warm, light-weight, shrink-resistant, hard-wearing, and moisture-resistant.

Most man-made fibers can imitate the appearance of natural fabrics. However, most man-made products do not have the flame-proofing of wool, the long-term durability of cotton and linen, the luxuriousness of silk, or the natural body-insulating qualities of wool, cotton, and linen. With repeated laundering, artificial fibers have a tendency to pill (formation of tiny lint balls on the surface of the fabric). Nylons and polyesters also tend to build up static in the clothing, and the clothes themselves sometimes cling to the body. However, there are sheets available that you can put in the drier with your clothes to prevent the static. Man-made fabrics that are heat-set (stabilized yarns and fabrics made of heat sensitive fibers) have the problem of setting creases and wrinkles from washing and ironing. Also, man-made fabrics do not breathe because of their low moisture absorbency.

4.   <u>Is it basic in color?</u>

When you first begin our basic wardrobe, try to stay with one color for the monochromatic look, or two complementary or contrasting colors for the mix-and-match mode.

Some good basic colors to begin with might be the beiges, the blacks, or the whites, or a combination of any two of these colors. For example, if you owned a pair of shoes, a handbag, and a pair of pants in beige and another pair of pants in black, you could collect your blouses and sweaters in any number of colors, fabrics, and styles to coordinate with the two pairs of slacks, and the shoes, and handbag, and create a myriad of different looks.

I personally do not believe in spending a lot of money on clothes. My advice to women who want to keep their wardrobe updated and look ever fashionable: Limit your wardrobe both from a color standpoint and the number of pieces, except for tops. There you can just keep adding in different colors, fabrics and styles.

I often see articles and documents in women's magazines whereby a basic wardrobe of one basic dress, two skirts, two pairs of pants, two jackets, four tops, and one V-neck cardigan in two complementary colors, say, red and black, for the skirts, pants, and jacket, and four coordinating colors, say, beige and white, for the tops, will enable you to create literally over a hundred different outfits from the twelve items of clothing just by creatively mixing and matching.

I have a businesswoman friend whose basic wardrobe consists of three pairs of classic straight-leg pants: one pair in black gabardine wool, one pair in beige wool crepe, and one pair in black raw silk; two jackets, a camel hair wool blazer and a black raw silk blazer; one pair of black leather pumps; and a black leather shoulder bag. She collects silk tops and sweaters in all different colors that coordinate with both beige and black (basic, neutral colors) and creates an endless variety of outfits for day and evening wear throughout the year. She always looks well dressed.

There was a time when color combinations such as blue and green (must not be seen), red and orange, and red and purple were considered unacceptable. Today they are avant-garde – chic and fashionable – although not necessarily basic, unless these are going to be the only two colors in your basic wardrobe.

Use color to create a mood. On a gloomy, cold day, wear bright, warm colors, such as red or orange, or both together. In the springtime, wear warm, fresh pastels, such as pinks and soft yellow.

Wear color to enhance an occasion. For a festive gala, wear merry colors, such as reds and greens. For a serious business conference, wear conservative colors, such as browns and greys.

Use color to denote a type. The pixie gamin type might choose the turquoises or shocking pinks; the futuristic type ahead of her time, the shiny, metallic-look fabrics in gold or silver; the extrovert, bright reds and purples; the business type, blacks and beiges; the athlete, whites and blues; the sultry type, shimmering blacks and whites.

I like and wear them all. For that reason I am particularly fond of stripes because I can indulge in all my senses.

5.   Is it comfortable?

Buy your clothes with comfort foremost in mind. Comfort before fashion is the keyword here. Women today are very busy, on the go. They need clothes that work for them; therefore, above anything else, their clothes must be comfortable.

It is senseless to wear those beautiful silk blouses in the summertime if you are among those who perspire excessively in silk when the cottons and cotton blends are much more comfortable during the hot summer months. And does the beautiful sequin-covered black dinner jacket warrant its discomfort and expense if you live in casual Hawaii? Or the mink bolero in hot New Mexico?

Avoid wearing your clothes too tight in the hopes of looking more slim because this technique only accentuates your size and gives the appearnace of your being overweight for the clothes.

In buying your clothes for maximum comfort, move your arms all the way forward to make sure the sleeve area is roomy enough and does not restrict your arm movements. Likewise, your pants should fit so that you can sit in them comfortably.

Fabrics often determine comfort. Cotton is most comfortable during the hot summer months because it breathes, as mentioned earlier. Polyester launders easily, but is uncomfortable to wear in hot weather because it does not breathe. One of my biggest mistakes in buying clothes was a 100% polyester tennis outfit in Southern California. Conversely, angora wool is very warm and may be comfortable to wear in Canada during the winter months but very uncomfortable in Southern California where temperatures range from the mid-seventies to the nineties in the winter months.

Probably the apparel that most frequently causes discomfort comes from the shoes, whether from an ill-fit or too much walking on high heels. Those high-heeled sandals and slides are beautiful but a pair of good, comfortable walking shoes with medium or low heels are a must in every woman's basic wardrobe. And remember, tired and sore feet reflect accordingly on your face.

In some parts of the country those beautiful velour and terry jogging suits are very fashionable and comfortable, and can be worn with your jogging shoes. If you are going to be shopping all day, do consider your utmost comfort which fortunately is so easy to achieve because we women have so many choices of outfits to wear. You need not be a jogger to wear the suit any more than you need to be a Moslem to wear harem pants.

In some rare parts of the country it would be acceptable to wear a tennis outfit and tennis shoes for comfort and shopping during the hot summer months, even if you are not playing tennis that day. I am fortunate that I live in such a community, although only a few minutes away from my home base I would look very conspicuous were I to enter a department store in such attire.

6.   How many different ways can I wear it?

The more versatility you can get from your garments, the more wear you will get out of them, and the more ensembles you will be able to create. Designer Geoffrey Beene is among the most versatile designers in that many of his clothes are designed to be worn different ways. For example, a poplin raincoat reverses to a plaid mohair coat; a lightweight jacket so simple it can be worn as a sweater; a smocked mohair coat that can be belted to look like a dress.

Buy wool or cashmere cardigans that you can wear day or night as a jacket, or buttoned up as a pullover (with the buttons in front or back), or tied around your neck as a middy.

Wherever possible, buy reversible clothing. Raincoats, chanel jackets, windbreakers, boleros, and wrap-around skirts are popular reversible items. Raincoats and windbreakers are sometimes available with a hood that can be folded to look like a collar when not in use, adding to the versatility of the garments. Particularly practical is the reversible poplin car coat with hood because it can be worn year-round as an all-weather coat and you need not be concerned about the hemlines changing with the seasons. Where winters are severe, consider an all-weather coat with zip-out lining.

Buy your first pair of boots in neutral leather that you can roll up or down to wear as the short boot, as the western look, or as the fashion mode.

Consider tops that you can wear under or over your pants and skirts either belted or unbelted. If you have a safari blouse with a matching sash, you can wear the blouse over your pants and belted, or under your pants looping the belt through the belt carriers of your pants, or you can tie the belt around your forehead for the western or prairie look. If you have a classic shirt blouse with matching detachable bow tie, consider wearing the blouse without the tie, or utilize the tie with your shirt blouse the same as you did the safari blouse.

The peasant blouse can be worn on the shoulders for the casual look, or off the shoulders for the formal mode. The Chinese mandarin blouse and jacket can be worn as street clothes or as lounging or hostess garments. Consider wearing a man's shirt as a tunic, belted or unbelted, over your skirts, pants, or leotards.

The prairie skirt that buttons from waist to hem is an item that can be worn ad infinitum. It can be worn buttoned or partly unbuttoned in either position from right to left as either a casual or formal garment. Unbuttoned to the waist it can be teamed with one or several underskirts of varying fabrics and lengths. If the western jeans and related accessories have been classic for two hundred years, there is no reason why the prairie skirt cannot be destined to become another American classic.

Some chiffon and lace nightgowns are so beautiful that you could wear them as evening dresses, especially the black or red ones. Just tie with a fringed gold rope at the waistline, unless the garment is empire waisted.

The first five points covered so far--seasonless clothes, classic designs, timeless fabrics, color, and comfort--also contribute to the many different ways you can wear your clothes. These points and the sixth point are related to the next question for discussion.

7.   How many different things can I wear it with?

Today women expect more out of their clothes, and rightfully so.

In these austere times, the disposable clothing era is gone. Women now want clothes that work for them and with them. Mixing and matching your separates is one way of getting the most value and versatility out of your clothes for a myriad of different ensembles to work for many different occasions for many years.

Two one-piece dresses in two different colors are essentially two different outfits that can be interchanged with sweaters, jackets, shawls, scarves, and jewelry.

Two skirt-and-blouse sets, each in a different basic color, such as black and beige that can be coordinated together or separately, will give you four different outfits that can be further interchanged with sweaters, jackets, scarves, and jewelry, as well as other pants, skirts, and tops, allowing you a very wide range of different outfits. The more ensembles you can create, the more exciting and practical your wardrobe. *That is modern.*

Unlike those one-piece dresses, your mix and match separates undoubtedly will be ensembles unlike any other fashion statement in the world. *Now that is creativity!*

Some jackets and raincoats, and occasionally skirts, are reversible, which allows the astute woman to instantly give her even more options to maximize her wardrobe possibilities. Boots are always a good choice with jackets and skirts because they add instant pizzazz to your wardrobe. I've even worn a smart ethnic tablecloth as a wraparound skirt. *And that is practicality.*

The classic suit jacket and the windbreaker jacket can be worn virtually with anything, everywhere, year-round. Both jackets can be worn for almost any day and casual night activities with anything from your classic Bermuda shorts to your classic

A-line skirts. In beige 100% cotton corduroy, for example, either jacket can team with any fabric from the denims to the raw silks.

The classic V-neck cardigan in wool or cashmere presents even more versatility than the Eisenhower jacket and the windbreaker because the cardigan can be worn year-round for both casual and formal day and night activities. It can be worn buttoned or unbuttoned with different colored blouses or pullovers, or it can be worn buttoned as a V-neck pullover, with or without accessories. It can also be worn as a middy over most of your tops by tying the cardigan sleeves around your neck in necktie fashion.

The traditional little black dress has unlimited versatility because you can dress it up or down with cardigans, jackets, and accessories. However, separates are the more versatile items because they can be mixed and matched ad infinitum. They enable you to create one-of-a-kind ensembles.

The best example of how many different things you can wear your garments with has been discussed in No. 4 -- Is it basic in color? Twelve items in two complementary colors (red and navy) were mixed and matched to create 122 ensembles. Had those twelve items been in coordinating basic colors, such as beige and black, or black and white, the range of different ensembles could be ad infinitum with the addition of just a few different colored tops.

There are many magazines that carry articles on how, say, fifteen key pieces of clothing can add up to 100 different outfits, clothes that you can count on for both day wear and evening wear, when you are traveling or wishing to expand your wardrobe. The key in creating the different ensembles is versatility: colors, styles, and fabrics that look elegant for both day and evening wear. Basic colors are the neutrals, beiges, whites, and blacks. For contrast and accent, choose the reds, blues, and greens, plus the pastels. Remember: get diversification from your tops – and accessories.

8. <u>How many different places can I wear it to?</u>

As discussed in the opening paragraph of this chapter, whatever clothing investments you make will depend on where you live and on your particular lifestyle. Naturally the sophisticated socialite in New York would have little use for casual California beachwear, and vice versa.

Classic jackets, tops, and cardigans in natural fibers can be worn to almost any activity any place in the world. Likewise, the shirt blouse in silk or cotton can be worn to casual or formal activities universally. I personally like a good silk or cotton shirt blouse as the key element in dressing, whether with an evening skirt or a good pair of jeans. All the natural fibers in solid colors have boundless diversification in that they are seasonless and can be worn virtually anywhere. Leathers and suedes can be worn to most day or night casual activities. And the black leather pants or skirt suit, made popular by the European designers, as well as jeans, can be worn to fancy restaurants.

In recent decades, according to Vogue, American and European designers have made popular and fashionable such clothes like the Chinese mandarin jacket, the African safari, the Russian Cossack shirt, the Indian caftan, and the American prairie and western apparel. In this jet age, there is apt to be an increasing trend toward ethnic costumes. Some of these designs are classics; others are destined to become classics; most of them can be worn internationally. In most recent years, clothing in leopard print has become a classic. As to what can be worn where in our versatile world of fashion was best said by dynamic New York designer Norma Kamali, who once said that even gray 'sweats' can be worn for evening wear with a great ruby and diamond necklace or fabulous silver cuffs.

9.   How is the garment to be cared for?

Fine clothes require fine care if you want them to last and remain looking good. The Federal Trade Commission requires that clothing made in or imported to the U.S.A. must be labeled as to their recommended care. Follow care label instructions careful. Bleaches should be use cautiously. Generally, it is safe to use bleach only on cottons and some of the cotton blends. Perspiration stains ruin clothes and weakens some fibers. Silks and wools in particular are vulnerable to perspiration stains; if your body deodorant is not effective against perspiration, try underarm pads. Ideally, silks and wools should be air-dried on hangers or laid flat on towels.

Wool fabrics should be dry cleaned and pressed with moist heat. Wool sweaters can be gently hand-washed with a mild laundry soap like Woolite in lukewarm water and

mild detergents, unless care instructions are indicated otherwise.
Wools washed in hot water and excessive machine agitation are subject to shrinkage and felting. Do not use bleaches or alkali. Wool
loses almost 40% of its strength when wet, but completely regains
its original strength when dry. If your wool clothing becomes shiny
from excessive wear, sponge with 5% solution of white vinegar and
steam; the fibers will swell and fluff. Wool and wool blends not moth-
proofed should be stored clean with camphor (moth balls) in con-
tainers with air vents. Too much strong sunlight or low humidity
causes the wool fibers to become brittle.

Although silk is strong and wears well, it requires special care.
Silks do not shrink but most of them must be dry cleaned; perspiration stains and excessive sunlight weaken the fabric. Some lightweight
silks can be very gently handwashed with lukewarm water and mild
detergent. Pure silks should be ironed damp under a press cloth.
Silk loses about 15% of its strength when wet, but regains its original
strength when dry. Silk should not be soaked, boiled, bleached, or
allowed to become too soiled before cleaning.

Although cotton soils and wrinkles easily, it launders well and
even boiling water and soap do not affect it. Most cottons and cotton
blends, as well as the synthetics, are best laundered in warm water
and mild soap, and tumble dried. If you do not like faded jeans, dry

of sending the clothes to special leather cleaners. Always seek personal recommendations about a dry cleaner from a reputable leather house or factory. Shop for a reputable dry cleaner for all your cleaning needs as you would shop for a trusting employee--with personal references carefully checked out. There are too many bad apples in the dry cleaning business.

Never, never allow your heels to get run down. Your shoes are your foundation. Invest in good quality shoes and take good care of them as you would your leather clothing.

Furs should be cold-stored by a professional furrier during the warm months. Yearly cleaning and glazing of your good furs will keep them new looking and prolong the life of your furs.

We all cannot have elaborate clothes closets like Zsa Zsa Gabor, but a well equipped, neat, and cheerful closet is a good investment and an incentive to take good care of your wardrobe. If you feel that your closet looks drab, try a cheerful wallpaper, or panel the doors with mirror tiles, or post a bulletin board on the door where you can keep an ever-changing gallery of fashion sketches, including your own creations.

Clothes should be organized: blouses with blouses, pants with pants, and so forth. Each type of clothing should be hung on like hangers for uniformity and neatness. To save space, consider the special skirt and pants hangers that hang vertically; that is, each hanger hangs down from the preceding top one. Clothing not worn during the current season should be cleaned and then stored in hanging storage bags especially made for the purpose of storage. Leathers and furs must not be enclosed for storage because they need to breathe to keep from drying out. Sweaters should always be kept in sweater boxes with vents for breathing or in drawers. Do not hang sweaters on hangers. It is a good idea to keep your delicate laces and velvets in a trunk. Belts should hang from a belt rack; scarves from a scarf rack. A shoe bag with vents or a wire rack for your footwear is a must. Wire racks are superior to bags and boxes because leather must breathe to keep from drying out. Delicate sandals and cloth shoes should be kept in clear plastic shoe boxes with vents. Purses should have an open shelf of their own. Fabric bags should be protected in clear plastic boxes with vents.

Finally, keep some camphor (moth balls) in your closets to keep the moths out of your wools. Be generous with perfumed sachets and potpourri in your lingerie and hosiery drawers.

10. <u>Does the garment reflect me?</u>

There is nothing so mundane as to look like, be like, think like, and dress like the general public, and then end up like a common garden variety nothing. Choose clothes that reflect you: your lifestyle, your special interests or hobbies, or simply your own preference of clothes.

Do not allow the clothes to wear you. It is acceptable to follow the fashion fads if this is what you want to do, independent of what everybody else is doing. However, the woman who selects her wardrobe only because it is "in style" for that particular season is not true to herself. The outer-directed woman who cannot wear anything unless it is properly labeled, on the outside of the garment no less, is so insecure that she functions not on her own approval, but rather on the approval of others. This type of woman is allowing the clothes to wear her. She believes in the cliché that "clothes make the person" rather than that clothes enhance the person. Fortunately most women today are too liberated and enlightened for that kind of superficiality. You know the clothes are wearing you when your friends consistently tell you, "Your outfit is great," instead of, "You look great."

There was a time when only the little black dress was acceptable for evening wear. Now women can wear anything from designer jeans to the business suit for dinner. Today's women also have the freedom to wear whatever skirt or pants length they wish. Gone are the days when women were enslaved to a dictatorship of ever-changing hemlines that necessitated buying a new wardrobe every season.

Today's woman can be her own real person. She can make her own fashion statement about who she is, not what a group of designers want her to be. With such a liberated outlook, today's woman can set the stage for her own fashion identity by producing her own scene changes. In a nutshell, she is her own individual, free, independent, unique.

11.   Is it an overall good investment?

The more positive reasons you can check off on The 12-Point Guide to Selecting Your Basic Clothes (Fig. I-1), the better the overall investment. A couture investment of $8,000 for an evening dress may not be a good investment if you should need to finance such a purchase over several months or years, for example, or if you anticipate wearing the gown only a few times.

Good quality clothes are not necessarily synonymous with designer labels. On the contrary, you are often paying for the prestigiousness of the label and sacrificing quality. Frank Doroff of Macy's New York recently said, "I don't think the name alone will sell anything any more. It depends on the product."

Given the same amount of money, it is better to buy a 100% cotton corduroy (natural fiber) Eisenhower jacket (classic style) that is well constructed and fully lined but without the fancy label than a 65% polyester/35% cotton corduroy (man-made blend) Eisenhower jacket that is unlined but with an internationally known designer label.

Recently I was shopping for a windbreaker and found one with a well-known California designer label in 100% lightweight cotton, beige and unlined, for $165.00. I looked at another windbreaker in the same store without any label on it in a beige 100% cotton poplin reversible to beige-and-white glen check in 100% lightweight cotton, for $52.00. Both jackets were otherwise well cut and constructed. For me the reversible jacket was the far better investment. For someone else the designer label may have been the important determining factor in making the purchase. This is fine. The important point for discussion here is that you need not necessarily spend a fortune on your clothes to get good quality.

That fashion reflects the times was recently confirmed by Geoffrey Beene who said, "I don't think women will be throwing pieces together quite as much at random. The look will be more put together, more studied out, more coordinated. I think that always existed with quality clothes, and with today's economy, while women are still dressing luxuriously, their sense of selectivity is becoming finer."

Many of our clothes are imported, making them sound investments if they come from countries where labor is inexpensive. This is especially true of handcrafted clothes such as hand knits, embroideries, leather weaving, and sometimes even hand-stitchery. Hand-embellished clothes are so rare today that even current works are becoming museum pieces. Is it a good investment to buy non-American? This is a controversial economic, social, and political subject. But remember my introductory remarks of this book: fashion reflects the times.

12. Is it an overall good asset to my wardrobe?

This last point is a compilation of all the previous guidelines discussed thus far. Most of us usually know at a glance if we are going to buy a certain garment or not. Many of these items are trendy, making them a poor investment in our economic hard times. If you want the most value for your money when considering your major clothing purchases, run a check of the garment in question against The 12-Point Guide to Selecting Your Basic Clothes (Fig. I-1). Some points will be checked 'yay' and some 'nay, ' but not all responses will carry the same strength. Therefore, I have included a sample of how to work a force field analysis, developed by Kurt Lewin, in conjunction with my twelve-point guide to help you weigh the value of any particular purchase you may be considering. The length (or strength) of each 'yay' or 'nay' response is a personal decision that only you can make. Let us take a hypothetical case.

Jane is a law student in California working her way through college. She lives on campus and is considering a designer label halter-top dress in black silk for $450.00.

The following work sheet illustrates how the twelve-point questionnaire (Fig. I-1) was forced into a field analysis, with the driving forces on a zero to ten plus scale and the restraining forces on a zero to ten minus scale. Fig. I-2 represents the results of this work sheet in graph form, which indicates that the garment would not be an overall good asset for Jane at this time.

1. <u>Is it seasonless?</u> Jane could wear the black silk halter-top dress in California year-round, except perhaps for a few very hot days during the summer months. (6)

2. <u>Is it classic in design?</u> The halter-top dress is a classic design which could probably serve Jane's needs for many years. (10)

3. <u>Is it timeless in fabric?</u> Given proper care, silk wears very well and retains its luxurious appearances for many years. (10)

4. <u>Is it basic in color?</u> Black is one of the best basic colors and works well with most other colors. (10)

5. <u>Is it comfortable?</u> Although the halter-top dress is comfortable to wear physically, Jane is thin and flat-chested; therefore, she feels the halter-top is somewhat uncomfortable to wear psychologically. (-7)

6. <u>How many different ways can I wear it?</u> The halter-top is a one-piece dress that can essentially be worn only one way. (-10)

7. How many different things can I wear it with? The halter-top dress does not lend itself too well to be worn with jackets or sweaters because these accessories would obstruct the design of the halter. A working student would better profit from an outfit with mix-and-match possibilities.   (-8)

8. How many different places can I wear it to? The halter-top dress would be suitable to wear to fine restaurants, the theater, and formal parties, all of which are limited in Jane's social activities and lifestyle as a law student living on campus.   (-7)

9. How is the garment to be cared for? Silk must be dry cleaned. Jane could better use the money toward more economical cleaning methods, such as laundry soap for cottons and linens.   (-8)

10. Does the garment reflect me? Jane is a working law student. The halter-top dress, although classic, would be more apropos for a socialite or a creative entrepreneur. A more simple, conservative design might be the better choice for Jane.   (-8)

11. Is it an overall good investment? Considering the strong minuses for questions 5 through 10, and the fact that Jane could better use the $450.00 toward her education rather than one luxury dress, this garment is not a wise overall investment.   (-8)

12. Is it an overall good asset to my wardrobe? Driving forces equal 36 points; restraining forces equal -56 points.

The -20 points does not make the halter-top dress in black silk

a good overall asset for Jane as a working student. . . . . (-20)

The 12-Point Guide to Selecting Your Basic Clothes

Whenever investing in your basics, ask yourself the following:

1. Is it seasonless?

2. Is it classic in design?

3. Is it timeless in fabric?

4. Is it basic in color?

5. Is it comfortable?

6. How many different ways can I wear it?

7. How many different things can I wear it with?

8. How many different places can I wear it to?

9. How is the garment to be cared for?

10. Does the garment reflect me?

11. Is it an overall good investment?

12. Is it an overall good asset to my wardrobe?

Fig. I-1

Fig. I-2

Force Field Analysis for

The 12-Point Guide to Selecting Your Basic Clothes

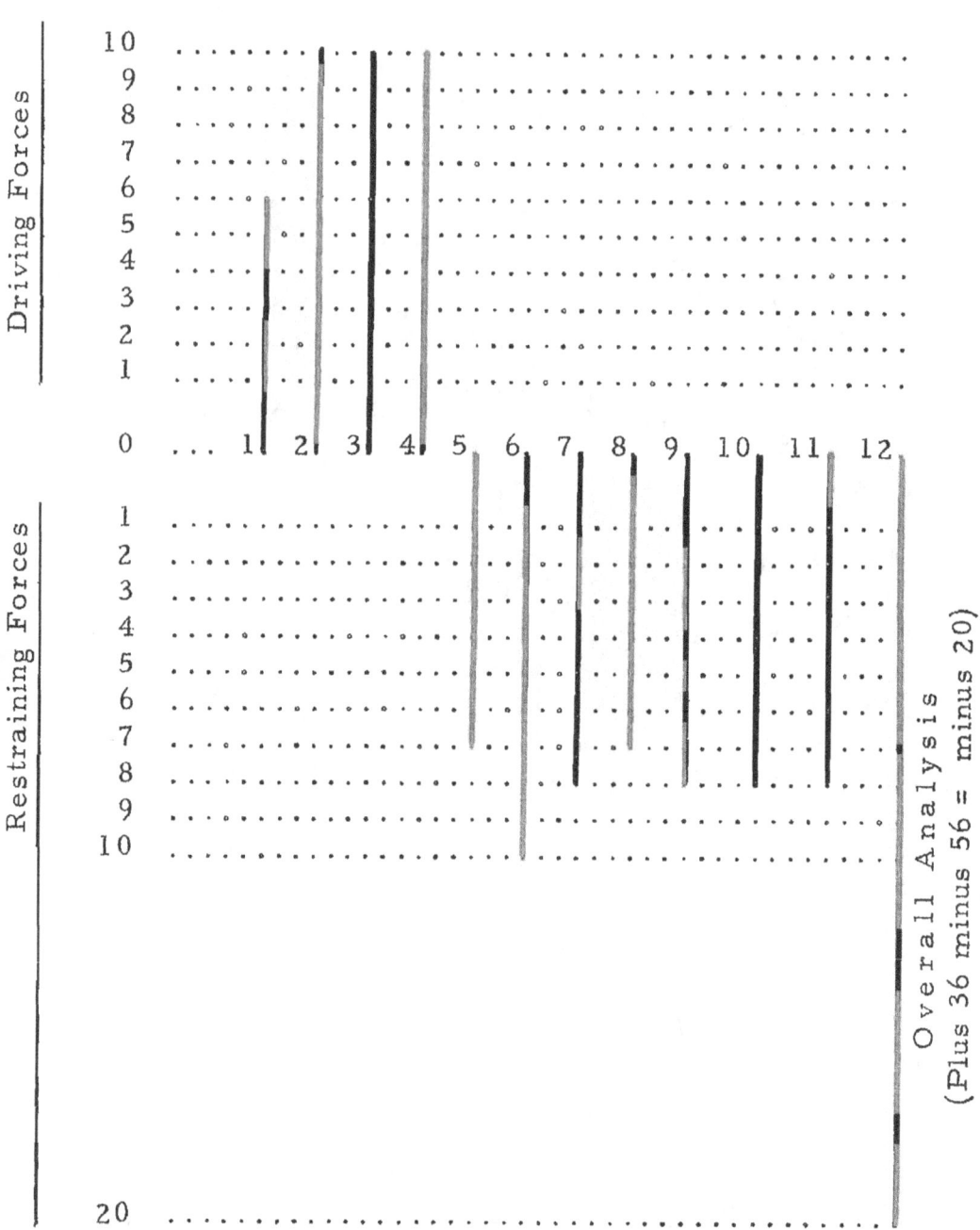

Chapter II

A Guide to Selecting the Basic Accessories

Accessories are very important in today's economic times because they help to extend your wardrobe by giving versatility to your clothes. Accessories work for us: they are today's fashion-makers.

Accessories are scarves and shawls, belts, and jewelry. Other pieces beyond your basic garments might include tops: jackets, sweaters, boleros and vests in basic neutrals, as well as coordinating and contrasting colors and textures. Still others are your shoes and handbags.

Whenever you are making major accessory purchases, use The 12-Point Guide to Selecting Your Basic Clothes (Fig. I-1) to determine if the piece under consideration would be an overall good asset to your wardrobe.

1. Scarves and Shawls

Your wardrobe of scarves can be unlimited. If you have a penchant for scarves, do try to keep these in silk to match your shoes or handbag, although preferably not both, unless you are dressing monochromatically. Scarves are very easy to make by pulling the warp and weft threads to get natural fringing (Fig. II-1).

If you are shortening a skirt, use the excess fabric for a scarf to achieve the designer effect (Fig. II-2). Or make a peplum belt to match your skirt and use it to dual as a ruffled lengthening border (Fig. II-8). Most any lengthening border can be used as a belt--see Chapter V, Fig. V-6 through Fig. V-10, and Fig. II-8.1 and Fig. II-8.2. Note that scarves can also be used to lengthen a skirt or top--see Chapter V, Fig. V-10.

See Fig. II-3 for the different ways to wear scarves:

(a) Wear your scarf around your neck, tied in a bow (Fig. II-3.1), under or over your blouse either long or short (Fig. II-3.2), tied or draped (Fig. II-3.3).

(b) Wear your scarf around your waist (Fig. II-3.4 through Fig. II-3.6).

(c) Twist it...around your neck to make a necklace (Fig. II-3.7); around your forehead (Fig. II-3.8); around your waist to make a belt (Fig. II-3.9).

(d) Wear your scarf as a headcovering (Fig. II-3.10 through Fig. II-3.12).

(e) Wear your scarf as a boot accessory (Fig. II-3.13) to add pizzazz to your footwear.

(f) Wear your scarf as a handbag accessory (Fig. II-3.14) for a splash of color.

(g) Wear your scarf as a bandeau (Fig. II-3.15).

Can you think of some other uses for the common scarf?

Shawls have become very versatile in recent years (Fig. II-4) and have been classic for several centuries. Apart from being used as shawls (Fig. II-4.1) they can be belted for the bolero look (Fig. II-4.2); they can also be draped around the waist (as can the square scarf) as an integral part of your skirt (Fig. II-4.3); they can be draped over your arms and around your shoulders to wear as an evening stole (Fig. II-4.4).

With some designs shawls can be used to create an ethnic look; for example, a richly colored paisley shawl with fringe over an ankle-length A-line skirt could start you off to the Cossack look. A popular European look is to drape the shawl over one shoulder and either let it hang loose (Fig. II-4.1), or tie it over the other shoulder.

You can also use steamer rugs (blankets) and linen and lace table cloths as shawls, which can be made into an instant skirt--just wrap around your waist and secure with a decorative pin (similar to Fig. II-4.3). Use natural fabrics and pull the warp and weft threads for a natural fringe (Fig. II-1) or you can sew one on.

2. Belts

You should have at least two leather belts in two basic colors to match your shoes. These should be approximately 1" wide. You can add versatility to your belts by selecting the kids that allow for inter-changeable buckles. A wise buckle choice for your two basic belts would be a solid brass one, and a matching leather-covered one. Ideally, the two basic belts should match the shoes you are wearing.

However, do not wear shoes, handbag, and belt in the same color because you will create a choppy look with your accessories looking like they came stamped out from a factory. An exception to this would be if you are wearing a totally monochromatic outfit. It also would be correct to wear unmatching shoes, handbag, and belt, so long as they are in the same family of colors; for example, earth colors of beige, taupe, and rust. If you like the old wild west look a tan tooled belt with a collection of brass and silver buckles would give your jeans and cords a variety of looks. Western apparel has been an American classic for hundreds of years and concho belts, recently popularized, are destined to become an American classic just as western apparel has been an American classic for hundreds of years. With proper leather care your basic leather belts should last a lifetime. And remember that a good leather belt can upgrade your clothing.

There are many different kinds of belts that are very easy and inexpensive to make and are so versatile that I have included illustrations on how to make a few (Fig. II-5). Fabric sash belts (Fig. II-5.1 and Fig. II-5.2) are practical year-round to match or coordinate with either your outfit or your shoes. Tapestry-like ribbons (Fig. II-5.3) likewise can be very easily made into belts. Spaghetti strings (macramé string) make a beautiful summer or fall belt (Fig. II-5.4), whereas multi-colored ribbons would make an interesting spring ribbon belt. Hardware chain belts can be used with or without further adornment (Fig. II-5.5).

For a funky look, drill holes through the tops of some seashells, affix a small metal hook or ring (available at hobby stores) and attach these rings to the rings on your chain belt like you would your charms on a charm bracelet. You can do the same with small pieces of driftwood, beads, or coins. You need not know elaborate macramé knotting to make a macramé and bead belt (Fig. II-5.6). However, if you desire an exotic design, there are numerous workbooks on macramé available at the library.

For a truly elegant and simple to make belt use fur (Fig. II-6.1). Join the fur pieces using an overcast stitching, as indicated in the illustration. Use commercially-made belt buckle and punch holes with a nail. Another elegant belt is made from feathers (Fig. II-6.2). Secure feathers to a fabric belt using the overcast stitch over each shaft of the feather. Using a fine needle and thread, work from bottom to top, as shown in the illustration. Use fasteners to secure the ends together.

You can also make your own simple leatherette or suede belts without leather tools (Fig. II-7). Make a simple sash belt with self fringe ends (Fig. II-7.1), or tie beads at the ends (Fig. II-7.2). Or use several very narrow strips of leather (approximately 1/4" wide) in matching or contrasting colors and braid a belt to fit your waist, leaving about twelve inch ends loose for tying (Fig. II-7.3). Or use grommets (available in kits at yardage stores) and ties to accessorize your leatherette belt.

Fig. II-8 depicts detachable borders that dual as a peplum (Fig. II-8.1) and a belt (Fig. II-8.2). Note that virtually any craft can be used for your detachable border to change your skirt from mid-calf to, say, knee-length, and give you a peplum or belt as a bonus. In my design (Fig. II-8), the grommets (available in kits at yardage stores) and lacings were used to secure the ruffles and the macramé and were made as an integral part of the total ensemble. Note that sleeves can be detachable in like fashion to change from long to short.

3. Jewelry

Not only is accessorizing with jewelry a very personal matter, there undoubtedly is no standard for basic jewelry. Like fabrics and leathers, your jewelry should be real, although your extended jewelry wardrobe can certainly be inexpensive, especially the new chunky pieces, many of which are made of natural products, such as brass and copper.

Traditionally, a simple strand of pearls could be considered basic because pearls are historically timeless: they can be worn any time, any place, with almost any thing, except sportswear.

An equally timeless piece of jewelry would be a 14K gold chain of somewhat heavy weight, like a three to four mm 18 inch rope chain necklace, for example. It would be even more versatile and certainly more practical (in durability) than pearls because it could be worn

permanently around your neck, if you wished, even with swimwear.
Furthermore, you could use the chain for your various pendants, charms,
and amulets to extend your jewelry wardrobe. The chain could also dual
as a bracelet by wrapping it a couple of times around your wrist. Again,
this bracelet could be used as a charm holder for a single piece of
jewelry.

For earrings, simple three mm 14K gold studs for pierced ears
could be worn at all times, if desired, and complement all your apparel
for whatever look you wanted to create, from the most conservative to
the most elegant, always simple, always in good taste. The gold studs
could be worn with either your pearls or gold chain, or without either
piece of jewelry. The pearls, gold chain, and gold stud earrings could
set a standard for your basic jewelry.

You could start your extended jewelry pieces by including a pair of
single pearl earrings. The collection of pendants, charms, and amulets
already mentioned could dual as jewelry pins by securing them with a
gold stick pin, which could be a jewelry piece in itself.

For practical reasons you will probably want, or need, a watch.
If at all possible, try to invest in a simple 14K gold watch. It should
be a lifetime investment and an heirloom.

The simple, unadorned gold band ring is traditionally a classic
piece of jewelry; however, the gold band is not always possible to be
worn by everyone. If a "diamond is forever," then your diamond ring,

if you choose to have one, could be your personal, basic, and classic piece of jewelry. A pair of diamond stud earrings set in 14K gold, even in 1/4 carat total diamond weight, could do a great deal to complement your diamond ring for evening wear.

To wear jewelry in good taste you need not invest a lot of money, so long as you keep the pieces natural and simple. Silk grosgrain ribbon for neckwear can be complemented with a small gold pin or simply a wooden bead. Macramé and seashells and wood beads make beautiful jewelry. With silk scarves being the price they are, you might even think of them as necklaces. You can twist the scarf to tie around your neck as a necklace for a jewelry piece (see Fig. II-3.7).

If you have a collection of charms and amulets, you can use silk cord or ribbon as a necklace. Your charms can be anything from 14K gold or sterling to seashells, driftwood, or feathers.

Some belts, such as silver and turquoise concho belts or foreign coins belts can be a piece of extensive jewelry in itself, without further adornment. See previous heading on Belts.

It is better to wear a real silk grosgrain ribbon tied around your neck than a gold plated or washed or flashed or whatever imitation piece. Jewelry should be an understatement; it should never overwhelm the wearer. Too much of even the most expensive jewelry takes on an overall gaudy, cheap look. An exception to this would be if you are very tall and statuesque, the type who can get away wearing a collection of

bangles, or two to three heavy gold chains --but not those skinny chains--
to create an exotic, bold look. However, you will notice that the top
international models, the world's most beautiful women, and the top
ten best-dressed women wear very little, if any, jewelry because they
do not want jewelry to detract from their beautiful bodies.

4.   Tops

I am including tops as accessories because beyond your collection
of a few pieces in classic designs and basic colors, your tops in varied
colors can work as collector pieces against a basic background of your
basic pants and skirts. For example, if you have three pairs of pants:
one pair in black wool gabardine, one pair in beige wool crepe, and
one pair in black raw silk, you have your basic pants. Add to that three
basic tops: one a long sleeved shirt blouse in beige silk, one long sleeved
shirt blouse with detachable bow tie in black silk, and one black V-neck
cashmere cardigan, all for your basic tops. These six pieces would
allow you up to nine different ensembles because beige and black coordinate well. From here on you could get numerous diversifications
by collecting any other colored tops or sweaters because beige and black
are both basic colors that coordinate with almost any other colors.
Your accessory tops can be anything from cotton tunics to team with your
wool pants to jewelry-embroidered sweaters to go with your wool or
silk pants.

Your accessory tops could also include all your jackets, although you should have one or two basic jackets to team with your basic pants. Good choices for basic jackets might be a camel hair and a black suede, both classic blazers. Both can be worn year-round, day and evening.

Separates have become very popular because they can be worn not only with different pants and skirts, but also with other category tops, such as sweaters and jackets and vests with blouses and other sweaters. Many of these separates can be worn different ways, as discussed in Chapter I; they can also be diversely accessorized, as discussed through-out this work.

5. Footwear

Body language psychiatrists tell us that our feet are power symbols that speak a non-verbal language. Therefore, it would behoove the well-dressed woman to be well heeled. And fashion experts claim they can tell a woman by her shoes.

A simple, conservative, medium- or high-heeled pump in fine quality beige leather can be worn all year round with most of your day and evening clothes. A second pair of simple pumps in black would help you vary your two-color basic wardrobe and accessories. The second pair of basic pumps could be a T-strap classic pump. You should also have a pair of simple low-heeled pumps or oxfords in one of your basic colors that could be worn year round for those days when you will need to stay on your feet most of the day.

Always keep your shoes well polished at all times. Dirty or worn down shoes are a sign of irresponsibility and weakness. Your shoes are the foundation of who and what you are. They are the most basic part of you.

If you are a sports or exercise enthusiast, again, invest in the best quality footwear for the occasion. Here the various socks--footlets to leg warmers--can greatly accessorize your footwear and body clothing.

An extension of your shoe wardrobe might include a pair of comfortable, low-heeled sandals for those hot summer days. Again, these could be worn with most of your summer clothes. Off-white leather would be a good choice of color. For the winter, a pair of versatile boots could be worn with most of your day clothes. I own a pair in off-white that go with all my Southwest (western, Indian, and prairie) outfits, even casual street suits, skirts, dresses, and jumpers, and every variety of pants from culottes to leather pants. They are knee-length height, but can be rolled down to the short boot that is so popular with the Indian and the prairie look skirts. At knee-height, I can wear them over my slacks to give them the knicker pants look. They also look great with wool skirts and jumpers. To westernize them, I wear the medium height, with add-on spurs.

Although your three pairs of basic shoes can certainly be worn year-round in the evenings, when planning your extended wardrobe you undoubtedly will want some elegant evening shoes. A pair of high-heeled simple pumps or sandals in metallic leather--gold or silver, or gold and silver--would be a good choice for any evening wear year-round. A pair of high-heeled simple pumps or sandals in black poi-de-soie with matching evening bag could be worn with most of your evening clothing. Because I am very fond of color in my clothes, I have a pair of high-heeled poi-de-soie sandals with black heels and sling back ankle strap, and multi-colored silk grosgrain ribbons across the vamp in my favorite colors of red, purple, green, and pink. They go with any of those colors all year round. They are my basic evening shoes.

If you live in an area where there is considerable rainfall or snow-fall, invest on protective footwear accordingly. Again, look for not only practicality but also versatility. I own a pair of low-heeled leather-look rubber and satin boots in the lumberjack style in maroon, lined with genuine sheepskin. These boots are practical because even if there is a hint of possible rain for the day and I am on an all-day outing, the boots dual as western boots, without anyone realizing that I am wearing rain boots. For versatility, they can be turned down to expose the sheep-skin lining. I have even worn mine to stroll along the beach on cold winter days.

6. <u>Handbags</u>

Two simple handbags in your two basic colors to match or comple-ment your three pairs of basic shoes is all you need to get your handbag wardrobe started. These should be in the finest quality leather you can afford because with care, they will improve with age, like fine wine, and

last for several years. Designer handbags are either of fine quality
or mediocre quality. However, the handbags that ostentatiously ad-
vertise that they are designer, like the ones with the signature or initial
patterns all over the bag look cheap and reveal the owner's obvious in-
security. It is important that your handbags be scaled to your body
build. For example, if you are a 5'-0" petite build, avoid over-sized
handbags, and vice versa.

Finally, have one good leather wallet to hold your money and credit
cards to put into your bandbags. Choose a basic color like beige or
black to go with either handbag, or something off beat, like red, that
becomes your trademark.

For the summer you might like a lightweight canvas or straw, but
this is not necessary for a basic wardrobe.

When extending your wardrobe, an evening bag is nice if you are
wearing evening shoes. Evening bags are so simple, yet can cost about
the price of a good leather bag that I decided to design my own and share
the pattern with my readers (Fig. II-9). The pattern is for an evening
clutch or shoulder bag and is especially elegant in doeskin, although pin-
wale corduroy or velvet may also be effectively used. From this
pattern you can also make a day shoulder bag using either medium- to
heavy-weight fabrics (cottons or linens) or even soft leather to wear
with your western, Indian, and prairie outfits, as well as the casual
street or sporty look clothes.

7.   Special Collections

Collect something that you particularly like, that expresses you as an individual, rather than someone else's "look." Your collection could be silk blouses, ethnic caftans, leather clothes, Indian jewelry, handknit wool sweaters, or whatever you enjoy wearing. If you have a strong sense of history and have an affinity for the American West, you might like to collect belt buckles or boots to accessorize your western wardrobe. Your collection then would be a reflection of your interest in and knowledge of the West. A friend Marge is from Arizona where she worked with the American Indians. Not only does she collect Indian jewelry, she learned how to make her own silver and turquoise pieces. Today she is in the Indian jewelry making business for herself. My daughter Kimberlee, thirteen, is a hat freak, and is known around the Palos Verdes peninsula for her unusual character hats. I like anything in leather and suede. Invest in and collect your fine clothes and accessories like you would your fine art treasures--to last a long time, even a lifetime. Let your clothes closet be your gallery. Let your wardrobe be your mirror, for your clothes should reflect you and only you.

Fig II-1- How to Make Scarves

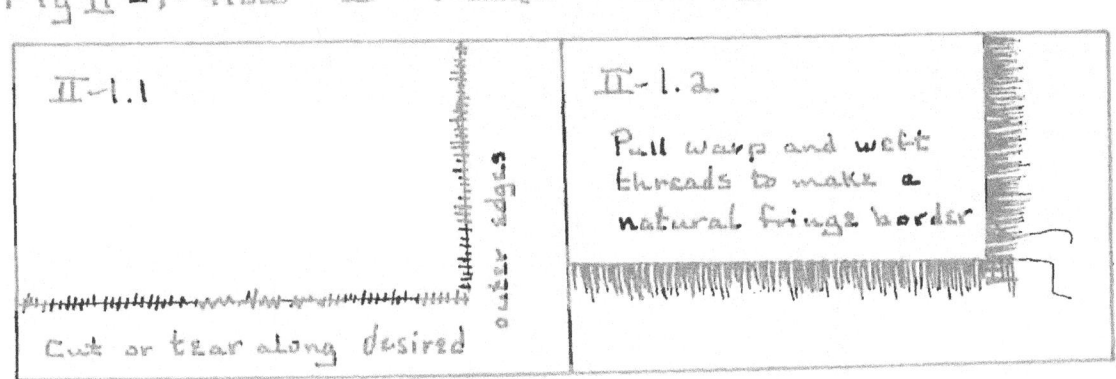

II-1.1

Cut or tear along desired

outer edges

II-1.2.

Pull warp and weft threads to make a natural fringe border

Fig. II-2- How to Make a Scarf from Shortening a Skirt

To shorten your skirt cut or tear off border to make a natural fringe hem and scarf for balanced look

Fig. II-3- The Different Ways to Wear Scarves

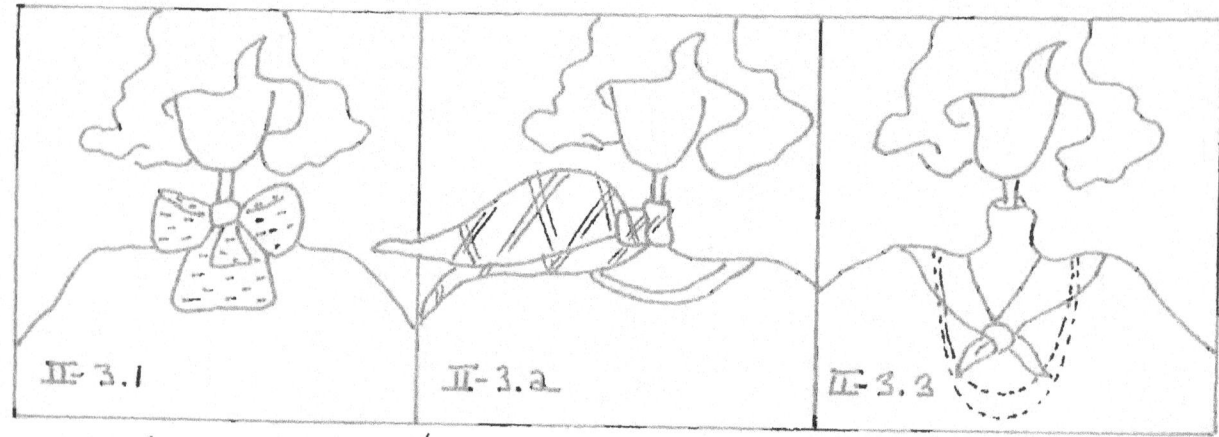

II-3.1   II-3.2   II-3.3

(a) Around the Neck

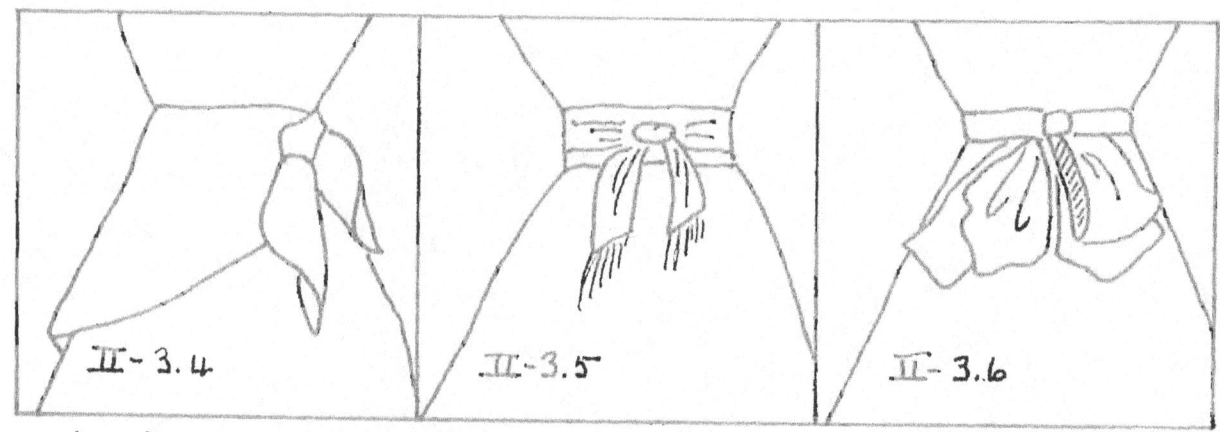

II-3.4   II-3.5   II-3.6

(b) Around the Waist

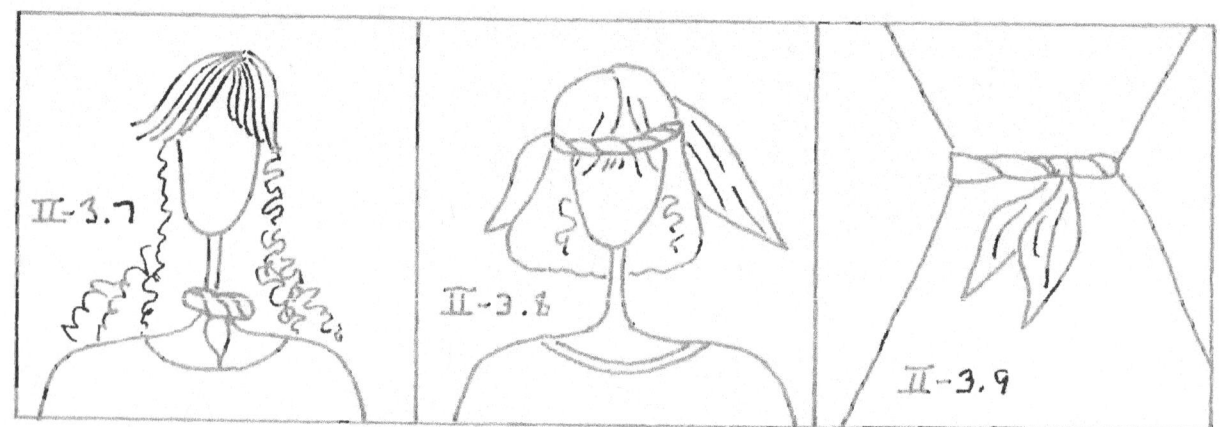

II-3.7   II-3.8   II-3.9

(c) Twisted... around the neck, the forehead, the waist

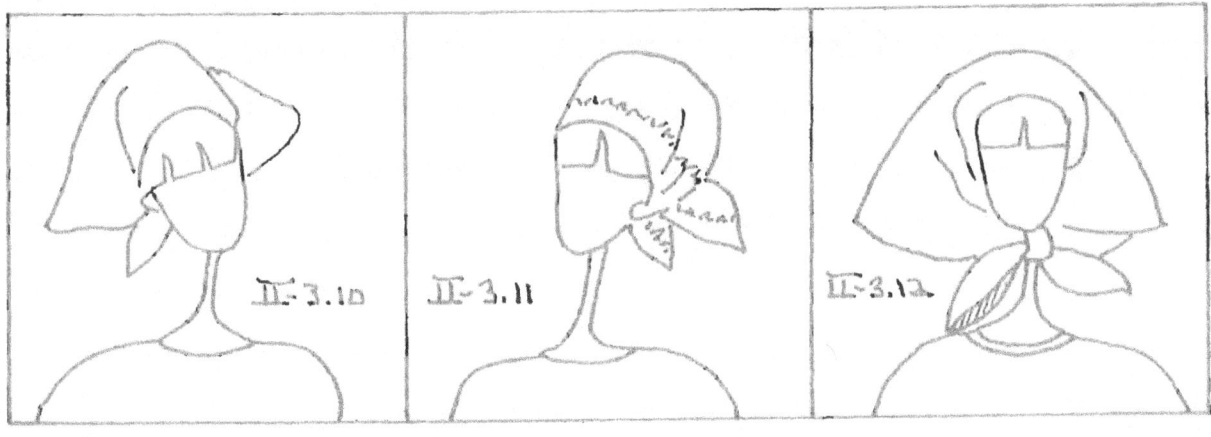

II-3.10   II-3.11   II-3.12

(d) As a Head Cover

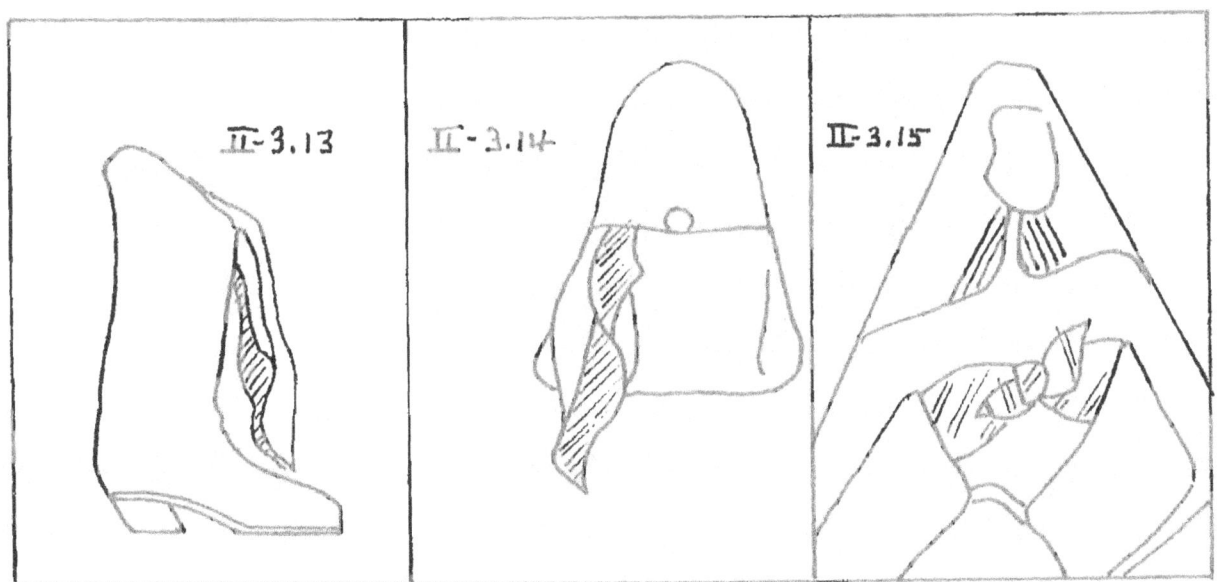

II-3.13   II-3.14   II-3.15

(e) As Boot Accessory (f) As Purse Accent (g) As a Bandeau

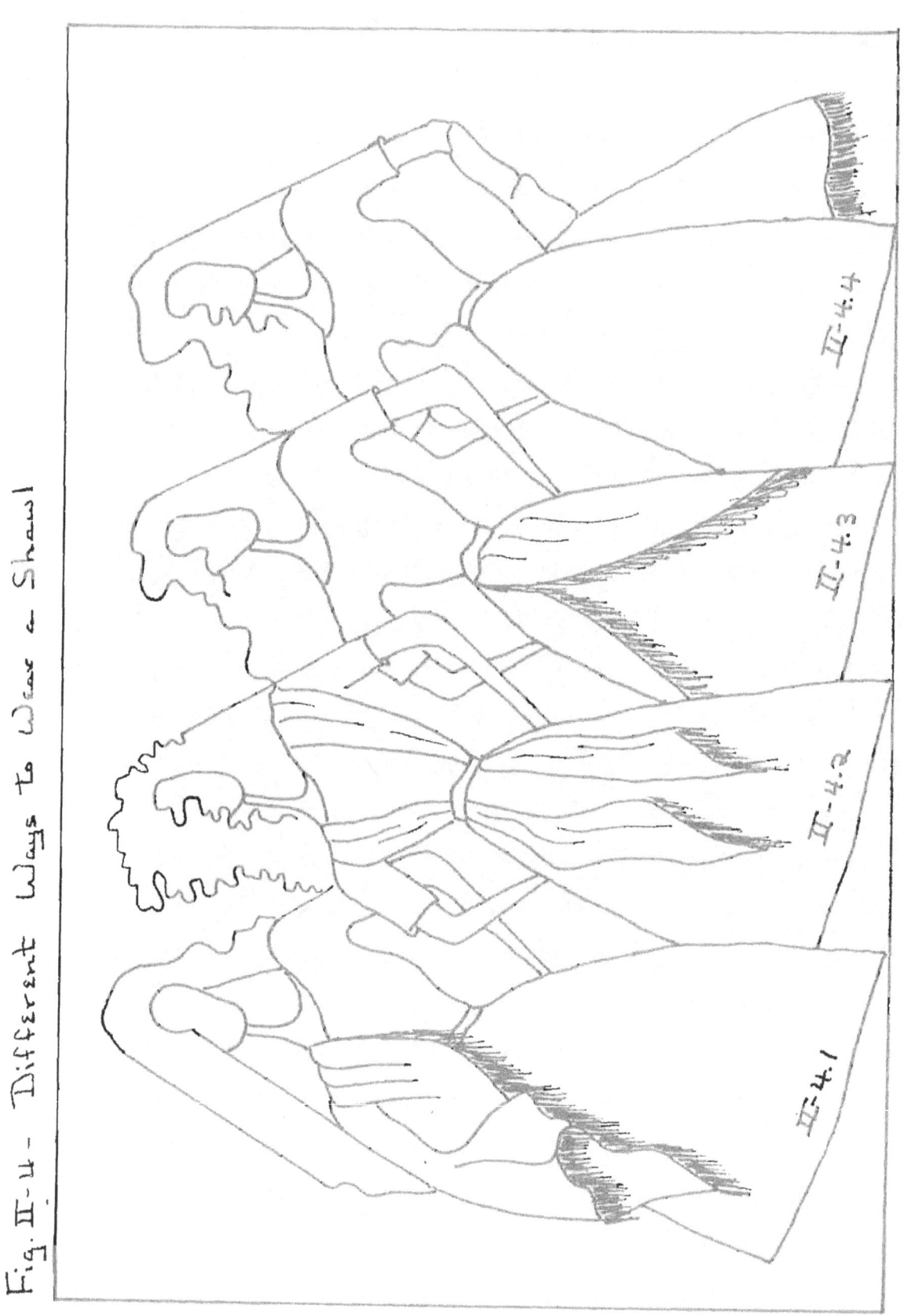

Fig. II-4- Different Ways to Wear a Shawl

II-4.4

II-4.3

II-4.2

II-4.1

Fig. II-5- Simple Belts to Make

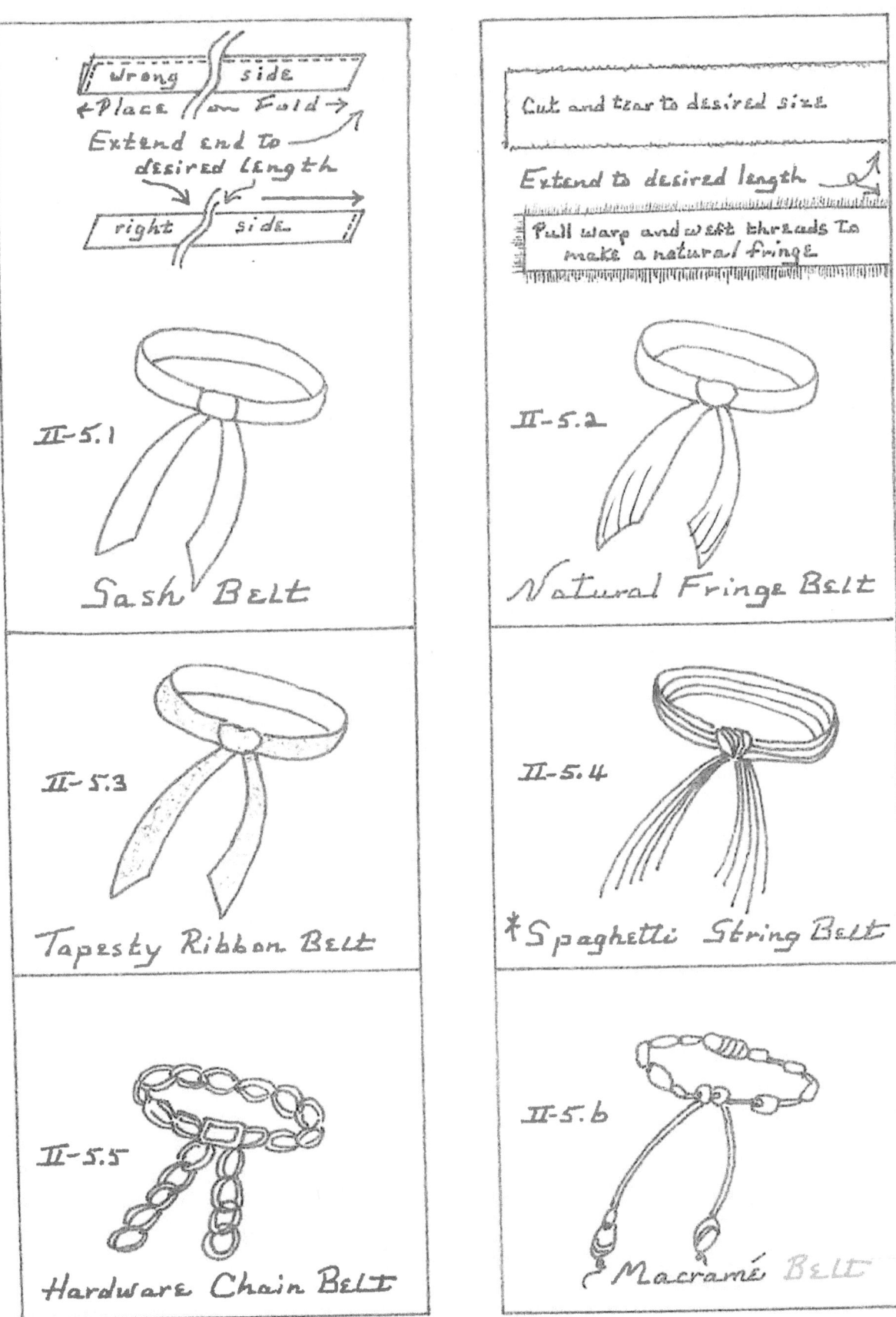

wrong side
←Place on Fold→
Extend end to
desired length
right side

II-5.1 Sash Belt

Cut and tear to desired size

Extend to desired length

Pull warp and weft threads to make a natural fringe

II-5.2 Natural Fringe Belt

II-5.3 Tapesty Ribbon Belt

II-5.4 *Spaghetti String Belt

II-5.5 Hardware Chain Belt

II-5.6 Macramé Belt

* Ribbon may be used

Fig. II-6 – Fur and Feather Belts to Make

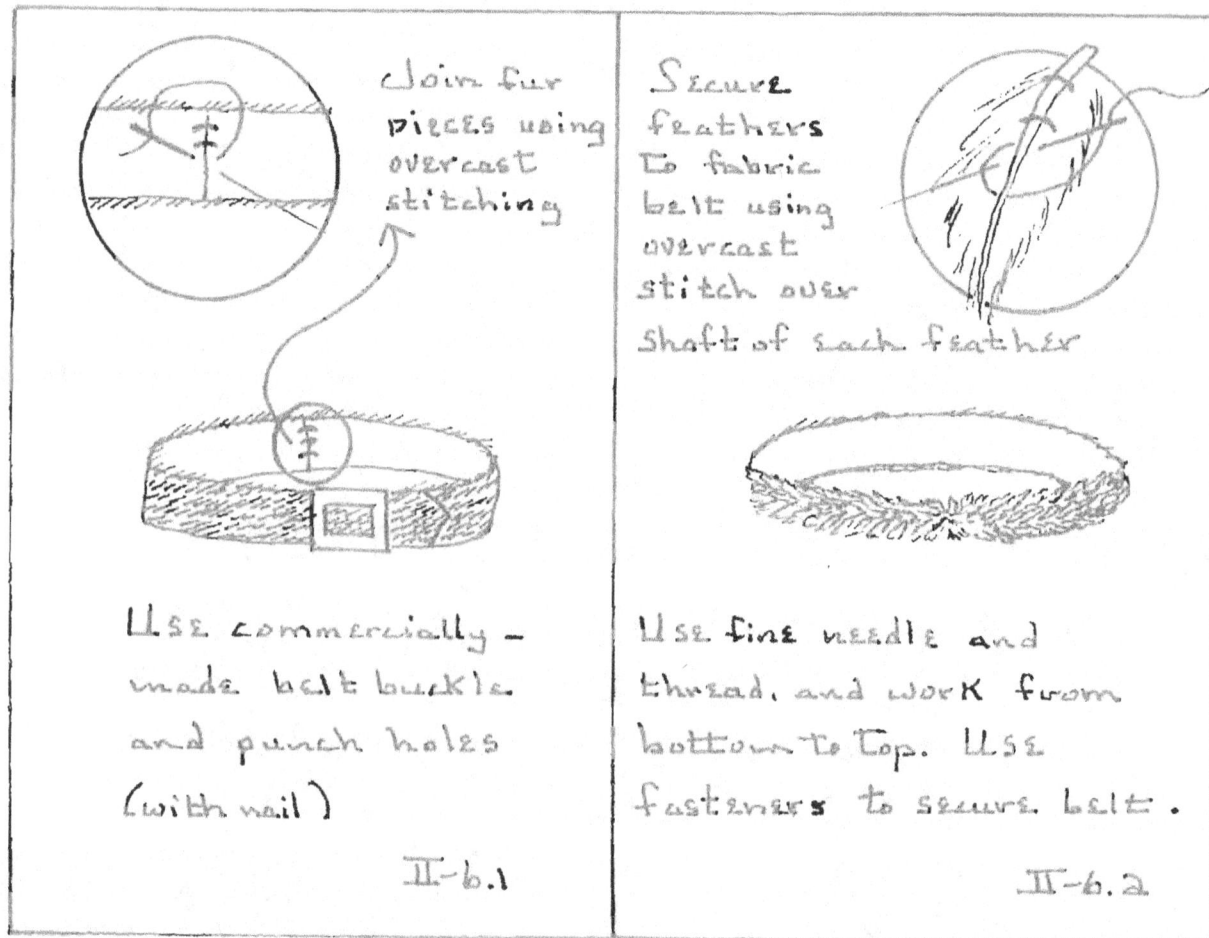

Join fur pieces using overcast stitching

Use commercially-made belt buckle and punch holes (with nail)

II-6.1

Secure feathers to fabric belt using overcast stitch over shaft of each feather

Use fine needle and thread, and work from bottom to top. Use fasteners to secure belt.

II-6.2

Fig. II-7 – Leather Belts to Make (without tools)

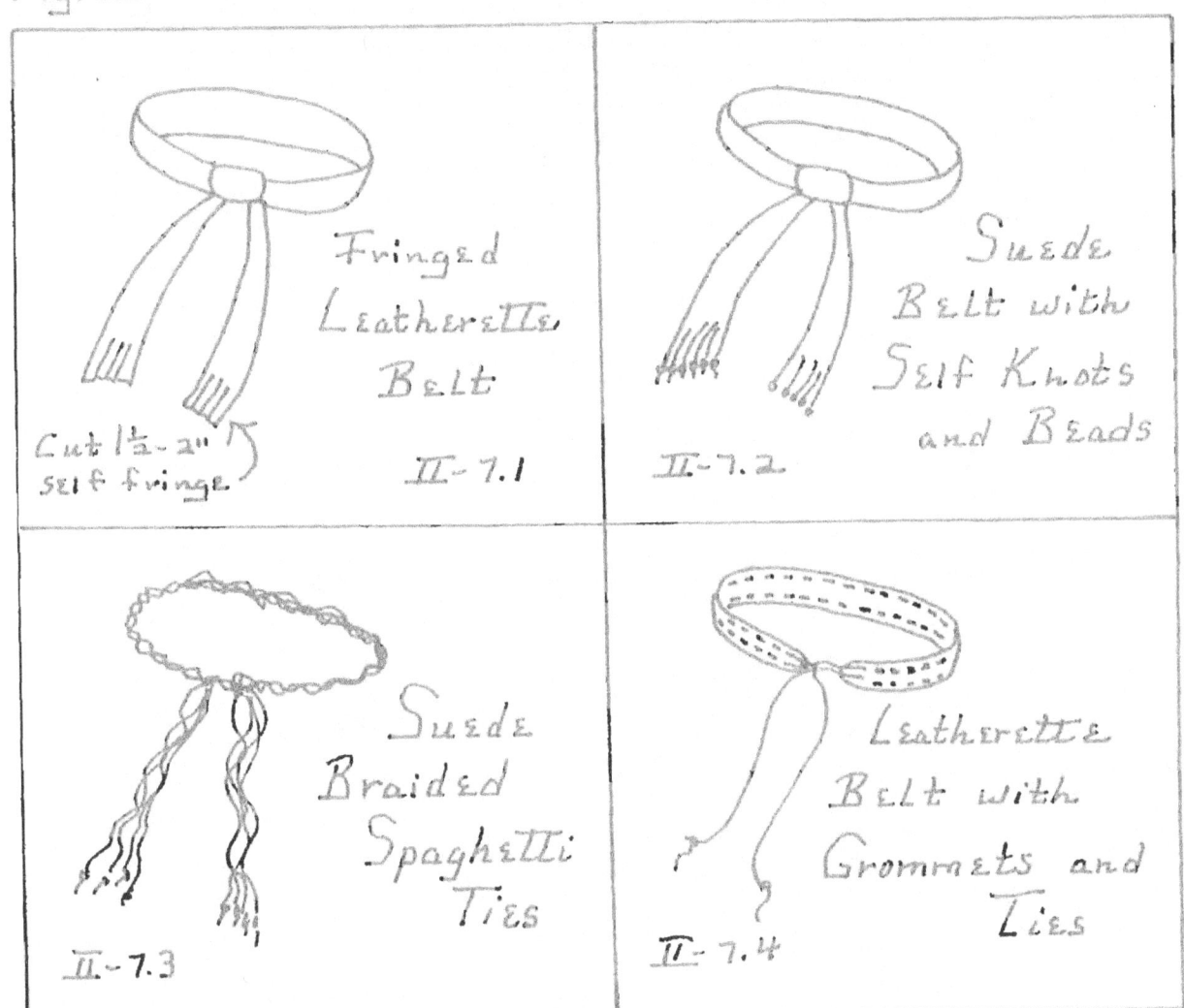

Fringed Leatherette Belt

Cut 1½-2" self fringe

II-7.1

Suede Belt with Self Knots and Beads

II-7.2

Suede Braided Spaghetti Ties

II-7.3

Leatherette Belt with Grommets and Ties

II-7.4

Fig. II-8 – Detachable Borders as Peplums or Belts

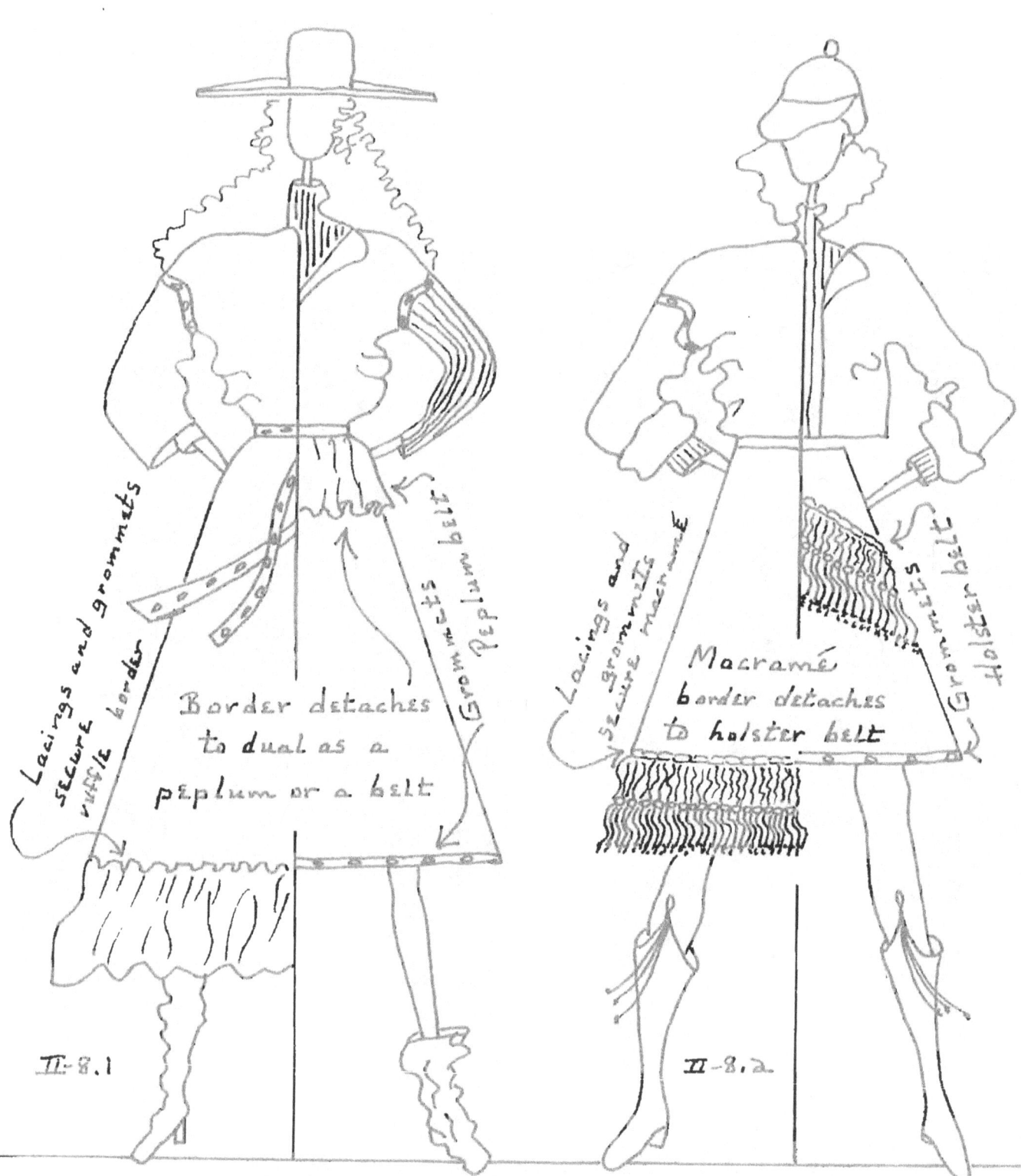

Lacings and grommets secure border ruffle border

Border detaches to dual as a peplum or a belt

Grommets Peplum belt

II-8.1

Lacings and grommets secure macrame

Macramé border detaches to holster belt

Grommets Holster belt

II-8.2

Fig. II-9 – Pattern for Clutch / Shoulder Bag
(not drawn to scale)

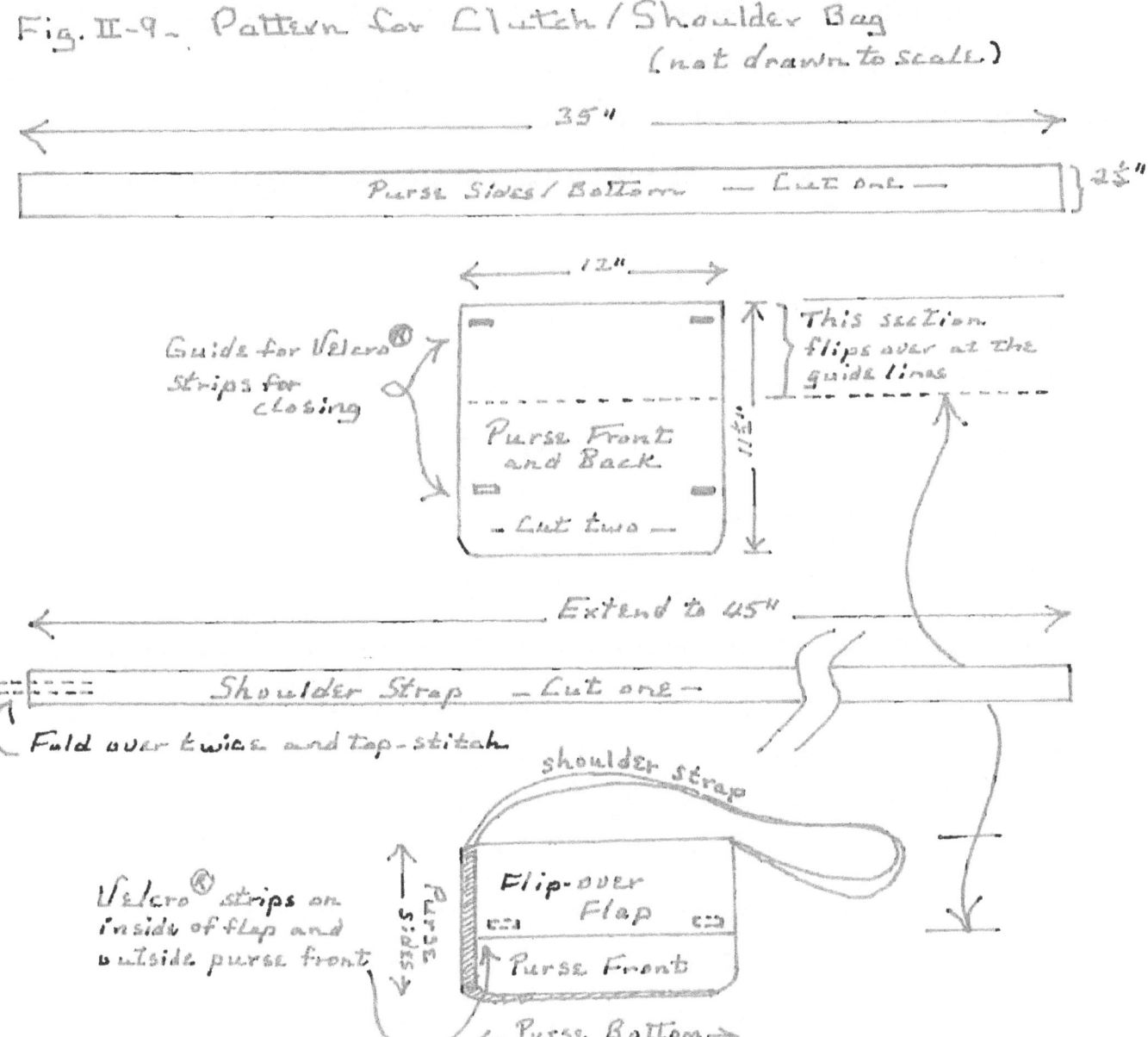

Suggested Materials: Soft leather, suede, or bargello
needlework on canvas. (Woven fabrics
require linings and additional seam
allowance.)

Chapter III

What Is Your Fashion Personality Profile?

Do you know who you are? Do you see yourself as your friends see you? Fashion is a mirror of your personality profile. But is it really your profile? Or do you blindly accept what Mr. Designer dictated you wear this year? Or do you wear whatever your movie idol wears? The foregoing profiles deal with the basic personality types: their characteristics, physique, fashion look. Also included are their choice of clothes, fabrics, accessories; first impression look; type of jewelry; hair style; what she likes to collect; her favorite designers. Each personality profile includes a key word that describes the total personality. See if you can pick out yourself. Then see if your friends can find you.

1.   The classic type

2.   The sophisticated type

3.   The business type

4.   The casual type

5.   The bold type

6.   The romantic type

7.   The glamorous type

8.   The sexy type

9.   The high fashion type

10.   The dumpy type

1. The Classic Type -

The classic type is the conservative woman who invests in her clothes to last forever, or at least a long, long time. Her clothes must work for her because she will not be a slave to her clothes. Today's liberated, free-thinking woman is apt to be the classic type. Her clothes are simple in style and cut, made from natural fabrics. Most of her clothes are seasonless, as well as timeless. First Lady Nancy Reagan is a classic type who, according to her press secretary, wears her old clothes all the time. Mrs. Reagan's hemlines have remained just below her knee for the past twenty years, despite the fact that hemlines have yoyoed from the mini to the maxi.

CONSERVATIVE

- pure, straight, uncluttered look
- gold jewelry and pearls
- natural fabrics in pure colors
- tailored suits and separates for day, elegant but simple silks for night
- simple hairdo
- tall and slim physique
- likes to collect classic designer separates
- favorite designers: James Galanos, Adolfo, Bill Blass, Yves Saint Laurant, Geoffrey Beene

2.   The Sophisticated Type -

The sophisticated type is a Renaissance woman: worldly,
cultured, intellectual. Her world runs the gamut from the arts to the
business sciences of making money--lots of it. Her wardrobe is not
typical because she enjoys a vastly versatile life style. Reversible
and seasonless clothes that work for day and night are a boom to her,
although her wardrobe includes classics from the simple and casual
sportive clothes to the glittering, glamorous designs, to the handmade,
one-of-a-kind artform pieces.

- strikingly beautiful facial and body features

- gold jewelry and pearls

- silks, cashmeres, and wools in neutral colors

- a range from casual, sportive clothes to elegant evening wear

- severe hair style

- lean, willowy look

- likes to collect beautiful jackets

- favorite designers: Halston, Gianfranco Ferrè, Claude Montana,

Geoffrey Beene, Oscar de la Renta

WORLDLY

3.   The Business Type -

The business type is fashionably all business and no nonsense. This type is the most practical in the fashion profile because she has no time to shop for clothes. Her clothes must work for her on the job and on to the evening for dinner, whether business or pleasure. Her clothes must be seasonless, versatile, and easy-care for her junkets, business trips, and "fact-finding" travels. This look is emerging strongly in the fashion world as more and more women enter serious careers rather than mere jobs.

PRACTICAL

- overall tailored look

- simple gold watch

- assorted wools, cottons, and silks in neutral colors

- two-piece suits, tunics, shirt blouses, turtleneck sweaters

- short, understated hair style

- medium height and build

- likes to collect shirt blouses

- favorite designers: Calvin Klein, Andre Laug, Liz Claiborne, Carole Little

4.   The Casual Type -

The casual type is the active, carefree, no frills woman. She is ever health-conscious and keeps her beautiful body in shape by regular gym exercise, sports, and jogging. She is usually synonymous with the California look. Because she is always on the move, she needs clothes she can move in. On cold days she wears leg warmers with her shorts and tank top. On the ranch she prefers blue jeans and plaid shirts. She is the down-to-earth, both-feet-on-the-ground type. The rest of the world thinks she is unsophisticated. But she knows who she is and needs not prove it to anyone.

- clean cut, tanned, athletic look

- very simple real jewelry

- leathers, tweeds, corduroys, denims, cottons, and cotton knits

- all kinds of pants, jackets, athletic clothes, T-shirts, Western gear

- short, blow-dried hair

- tall, trim physique

- likes to collect oversized tops

- favorite designers: Ralph Lauren, Norma Kamali, Giorgio Armani, Claude Montana

ACTIVE

5.   The Bold Type -

The bold type is the highly creative woman who is fashionably avant garde. She is worldly and enjoys shopping for unique and exotic clothes on research trips abroad. Of all the fashion personalities, the bold type is the most creative, inner-directed woman. She neither knows nor cares what is "in" or "out" of fashion because she thinks for herself and dresses accordingly. She creates her own style and charts her own destiny.

- daring, exotic look, or expressly unique style

- chunky and ethnic jewelry and belts

- fabrics in Eastern prints in contrasting textures and uninhibited

   colors and hand-painted designs; leathers and suedes

- bewitching laces, fringed shawls, stripes and prints juxa-

   positioned and collaged into bold ensembles

- untamed or exaggerated hair style

- very tall, statuesque physique

- likes to collect exotic shawls

- favorite designers: Michaele Vollbracht, Emanual Ungaro,

   Pino Lancetti, Georgio Sant' Angelo, Claude Montana

C R E A T I V E

6.   The Romantic Type -

She is very feminine and sentimental. When she travels she likes to bring back something to wear as a souvenir. Women's lib is not for her. She is the traditional type and all woman. She prefers to work at home where she can indulge in romantic flowing caftans by day and lounging pyjamas by night. She also likes to crochet and embroider and embellish her own clothes. Her fantasy and antique-look clothes are neither in nor out of fashion, yet always in style.

- everything soft in fabrics and pastels

- dainty jewelry

- nostalgic ruffles, laces, embroideries, and floral prints

- peter pan collars, poofy sleeves, full skirts

- soft, curly hair

- small physique

- likes to collect lacy Victorian tops

- favorite designers: Bill Blass, Perry Ellis, Zandra Phodes, Oscar de la Renta, Karl Lagerfeld (for Chloé)

SENTIMENTAL

7.   The Glamorous Type -

The glamorous type lives in a world of beautiful things and feels beautiful about herself. It is inevitable then that she would wear beautiful clothes. What would seem like unpractical wearing apparel to most women is common place to her. Diamonds are her favorite accessories. Her sparkling clothes are a reflection of her sparkling personality. Most of her clothes are elegant evening ensembles because she loves the night life, when she can glow and light up everything and everyone around her.

- razzle dazzle glitter look

- diamonds

- soft flowing chiffons, silks, velvets, and satins in black, white, red, or purple

- feathers and furs and sequins, gold and silver lamés

- curly hairdo, long or short

- tall, slender physique

- likes to collect beaded sweaters

- favorite designers: Carolina Herrera, Valentino, Bill Blass, Geoffrey Beene, Oscar de la Renta

SPARKLING

8.   The sexy type -

Her pretty face, volumptuous body, and ultra feminine mannerisms belie her intellect, which makes her doubly gifted in the world of fashion and career. Whether she wears a shirt blouse or a bulky knit pullover, she always looks sexy because her body transcends whatever she is wearing. She is the personification of everything feminine. Running a boutique business would be her choice for a career, although her wardrobe reflects her love of being at home either in the country or on the coast.

- very soft, feminine look

- no jewelry

- soft chiffons, maribou, and feathers in whites, reds, and pinks

- plunging necklines, slit skirt seams, bare shoulders, sandals

- soft, long hair

- curvy, volumptuous body

- likes to collect beautiful pignoirs and lounging clothes

- favorite designers: Bob MacKie, Valentino

FEMININE

9. The high fashion type -

The high fashion type follows fashion religiously. She is ever-conscious of what every label costs, but is often ignorant of its value. She needs clothes for emotional stability, to show the world that she has arrived, not through her own efforts, but through her husband or her father or her mother. Because she has no identity of her own, she cannot project any individuality into her clothes. She becomes then a counterfeit of someone or something else. Consequently, the clothes wear her.

- the "latest" trendy look

- diamonds or rhinestones

- designer fabrics in pure colors and natural fabrics

- religious following of the "in" trends

- modern hairdo

- short to medium stature

- likes to collect nothing because she must have a "new look" every season

- favorite designers: whoever the media's favorite idol's designers are at the time

COUNTERFEIT

10.   The Dumpy Type -

The dumpy look is the poor counterpart of the rich high fashion type. She prefaces most of her sentences with, "My husband...." or "My kids...." or "My parents...." Like the bloodsucker leech, she draws sustenance from and through another person or persons. She is dull, drab, and outer-directed. She can be heard saying, "Why can't you be like everybody else." Since she cannot think for herself, she must always follow someone or something, including the fashion fads. Fortunately for the rest of the women in the world, this type is becoming an endangered specie.

- dull, drab appearance

- plastic jewelry

- man-made fabrics in currently "in" colors

- the "latest" fad and trendy fashions

- short, mousy brown hair with no style

- fat

- likes to collect those handbags with the designer's initials or name all over them

- favorite designers: her neighbor's or her mother's

PART II

LET'S GIVE THOSE OLD CLOTHES A NEW LOOK

I have discussed in Part I how to select your wardrobe by using

the basic pieces of clothing and accessories. Theoretically, you

could be a well dressed woman for all seasons with this set of basics.

However, you probably have some clothes that you either no longer

can or no longer want to wear and would like to give them a new look.

Or, you like to follow the latest styles but do not want to throw out

perfectly good clothes and spend a fortune every season on a new

wardrobe.

Part II is replete with illustrations and simple directions to

help serve as an impetus in updating and even redesigning your old

clothes in order to diversify and extend your wardrobe. Fig. IV-1 -

The Family of Pants in Chapter IV is an excellent example of

illustrating in a nutshell how basic fashion design really is. Many of

the alteration methods for clothes and accessories described in Part II will help upgrade your wearing apparel considerably and make many of the pieces original, one-of-a-kind artforms. This is an excellent opportunity for you to be your own designer. It is also good conservation and economic practice. Check your wardrobe. Let your creativity flow. And learn to be your own couturier.

Chapter IV

The Family of Pants

From the classic straight leg pants there are over thirty variations in different lengths and widths. Further variations include one-piece pants outfits, such as overalls, jumpsuits, jogging suits, and a myriad of dress pants ensembles.

Let us assume that you have an old pair of straight leg pants still in fine condition but you are tired of them. What can you do with them? You can elasticize the hem for jogging pants; you can cut them down for western style pants, or for stretch or ski pants by adding elastic bands to the bottoms; you can drop the waist to make hip huggers; you can cut the legs of the pants to make: capris, clam diggers, pedal pushers, bermuda shorts, jamaica shorts, short shorts, jogging or gym shorts. Bell bottom pants can be made from straight leg pants by adding godets. Furthermore, by adding godets to your straight leg pants you can make any one of the wide pants (see Fig. IV-1 and IV-6.3). Conversely, from the widest group of pants you can make any one of the some thirty different pants illustrated in Fig. IV-1.

Fig. IV-2 illustrates how the hems can be gathered for some pants: jogging pants, knickers, knickerbockers, cossacks, balloon pants, harem pants, palazzo pants, and bloomers. These techniques range from the simplest (knotting, pinning, or tying) to the most complicated (cuffs), depending on how much time and effort you are willing to extend, or the look you are trying to achieve. Actually the simplest methods mentioned are the most practical because you can wear the pants as, for example, either hostess pyjamas or harem pants without making any permanent alterations.

When you are making cuffs, ties, or carriers for your pants and do not have matching fabric, use a contrasting color and repeat it in a tie belt or scarf for the balanced and designer look. Rope cording (Fig. IV-2.4) in gold also works well and may be repeated as a belt, or even as a bolo tie around your neck.

1.   Shortening Pants

The most conventional way to hem pants is to cut off the excess length and hem, and either iron on hemming tape (Fig. IV-3.3), clean them. Some cotton corduroys may be laundered at home; turn the garment inside out, wash on the delicate cycle and tumble or air dry. Cotton blends, such as cotton/polyester, are especially good for the busy career woman who does not have a lot of time for laundering or trips to the dry cleaners because the blends, or wash-and-wears, can be drip-dried without need for ironing.

Linen requires little care and can be laundered or boiled. With the crease-resistant resin finishes, linen needs little care. Stains can be removed from linen by pouring hot boiled water through the linen without damaging the fibers. To retain the luster of linen, the fabric should be ironed damp or with steam. Linen is resistant to bleaches and high temperatures, and more resistant to sunlight than cotton, wool, and silk.

Leather bags and shoes should be treated with leather cleaners and moisturizers according to the manufacturers instructions. Leather clothing should be cleaned and glazed by professionals. Most suedes can be sprayed with a suede protector to help repel dust and dirt, much as upholstery fabric can be Scotch Guarded for the same problems. Suedes can also be brushed with a special brush designed for the skin.

If your skins need professional cleaning, a word of warning: know your dry cleaner. Be sure that your dry cleaner does not attempt to clean your suedes by ordinary dry cleaning methods in lieu or use the stitch-and-overcast hemming method (Fig. IV-3.4).

Certain fabrics, such as denims and cottons, lend themselves well to simply tearing off the excess length (Fig. IV-3.3). For pants made of loosely woven fabric, the weft threads (running across) may be pulled for a natural fringe (Fig. IV-3.4). Both styles can be either Bohemian, when worn with an old, faded shirt, or avant-garde, when worn with a silk shirt blouse and chunky jewelry.

Use elastic thread and top-stitch two rows (about 6 to 8 inches) along the outer part of the pant legs for a dressy look (Fig. IV-3.5). This works well with lightweight fabrics, especially silk. Regular sewing thread may also be used, as illustrated in Fig. IV-3.5. First loosely top-stitch two rows on the wrong side and pull the threads to gather the desired effect. Then permanently top-stitch on the right side. Remove the gathering threads from the wrong side. The permanent top-stitching thread may be in a contrasting color, if you can repeat this color elsewhere in a top or an accessory.

You can give your pants dual lengths by sewing in a tab inside the pants, along the outer side seam of the pant legs. See Fig. IV-3 for placement of the tab (inside the pants) and the button (outside the pants). The tab can be made of a contrasting color, if you do not have matching fabric, but be sure to repeat the color in a self tie for your waist, neck, or head (see Chapter II for various accessory ideas).

2.   <u>Lengthening Pants</u>

One of the simplest ways to lengthen your pants is to use suede or soft leather (Fig. IV-4.1). Cut the fringe (about 2 to 3 inches) before you sew on the lengthening piece. Get enough suede or leather for a self belt (with self fringe), as well as a vest, if you sew well, or a self-fringed cape, if your skills are limited. And note the back pocket illustrated for these pants.

Let your creativity flow for a beadwork design (Fig. IV-4.2). There are several kinds of embellishments to choose from: sequins, rhinestones, eyelets, metallic studs, and a wide range of beads from wood to plastic. Most of these ornaments are also available in kits, complete with tools (if necessary), instructions, and even design patterns and ideas.

If you like to crewel embroider, consider working a piece for your pants (Fig. IV-4.3) for an elegant and expensive designer look. Never, never throw out anything, no matter how worn, with any embroidery on it because often at least a small section of the embroidery can be utilized for upgrading your old clothes, even if you can salvage only a piece small enough for a pocket. Old embroidered pillow cases can be recycled for lengthening your pants. Machine-embroidered fabric and small tapestries also work well. And monogram your own name or initials on a pocket in a coordinating fabric.

Patchwork lengthening (Fig. IV-4. 4) can be especially creative. You can make an assemblage of your own random patchwork using cottons, or you can create a "modern art" piece using satins and metallic fabrics. Refer to the circled illustration how to sew the patches together. For the scattered patches, refer to the circled illustration for border appliques (Fig. IV-4. 8). A patchwork self belt and pocket would coordinate well with these pants. There are also patchwork printed fabrics that you can use for this lengthening design.

For the collage design (Fig. IV-4. 5) use scraps of suede to create a scene on a suede lengthening panel. Use leather-to-leather glue for this piece and cut a self tie belt from the background color. Other materials you can use to make a collage are: felt, short hair furs, appliques (handworked or machine-made), laces and trims, campaign buttons, and fabric badges.

Michaele Vollbracht is a famous fashion designer who works exclusively with hand-painted designs on clothes. Fig. IV-4. 6 is an example of how you can too. Yardage supply houses have available special marking pens to use on fabric. If you are not an artist, little children are. Let them paint on a fabric piece that you can use to lengthen your pants (Fig. IV-4. 6). Or let them leave their little hand or footprints on the lengthening piece for their own

Grauman's Chinese Theater message. Acrylic, textile, or oil paint may be used. To clean the pants, the garment should be turned inside out and gently washed in lukewarm water.

Internationally famous designer Mary McFadden incorporates macrame into her couture designs. So can you. Fig. IV-4.7 illustrates a macrame hanging that you can wear. There are many volumes of books on macrame that you can use to help you create a piece for your pants. (Detailed instructions on how to make macrame are beyond the scope of this book.) Add a macrame belt. And be sure to use beads and long fringe in your pieces to add movement and excitement to your overall outfit.

Some border prints are readily adaptable to lengthening pants, particularly if they can be incorporated as an integral point in the design of the pants (Fig. IV-4.8). Parts of such a border print may be cut out and appliqued elsewhere on your pants. Cut approximately 1/4" around the desired design, position with pins and baste in place. Turn the 1/4" excess edges under and secure with tiny overcast stitching (Fig. IV-3.4) to secure the applique in place.

The eight lengthening hems discussed here should serve as a springboard to help you with your own innovative ideas. Whatever handcrafts you enjoy doing, you can incorporate into the design of your pants.

3.   Altering the Width of Pants

(a) Alterations for Pants Too Big - The simplest method of taking in pants is by stitching (on the wrong side) the desired width and cutting away the excess fabric (Fig. IV-5.1). You can extend the stitching into the belt, if the waist needs adjustment, although this will not give your pants the professional tailored look on the inside of your pants. If you are a perfectionist, remove the belt, make the required adjustment in the front waist band area, and re-sew the band.

Note what you can do with an old pair of jogging pants (Fig. IV-5.2). The fabric should be a soft, stretchy knit for the leg warmers. Make a casing for the top of the warmers and elasticize (see Fig. IV-2.2) to fit your legs.

If you need to take in only a few inches, say a 1/2" off each side of your pants, rip the side seams apart but do not press them out (Fig. IV-5.3). Cut through the waist band and finish the edges with a zig-zag machine stitch (see circled illustration). Working from the outside of your pants, overlap the front pant seams over the back by 1/2". Work a row of a running stitch in a contrasting color, or do a double row of a machine top-stitch to secure the side seams in place. Repeat the color of the thread in a top or an accessory piece.

(b) <u>Alterations for Pants Too Tight</u> - If your pants are too tight, say 1", cut two 1/2" (plus seam allowance) panels the length of your pants (Fig. IV-6.1). Open both side seams and press out. Cut through the waist band and finish the edges with a machine zig-zag stitch, as shown in Fig. IV-5.3. If you need to extend these edges to work with your side seams, use the contrasting fabric of the panel so that this part of the waist band will look like side tab openings. Insert the contrasting panel as shown in Fig. IV-6.1. Repeat this color (of the panel) in an accessory. See Chapter II for accessory ideas.

The use of side seam lacings is an innovative practice for widening your pants (Fig. IV-6.2). Cut through the waist band and rip the side seams apart as for the pants in Fig. IV-6.1. However, do not press out the seams; machine zig-zag the edges of the waist band (Fig. IV-5.3). Follow manufacturer's package instructions to apply the eyelets, which usually come complete with the required tool. The eyelets should be spaced 1 to 1-1/2 inches apart. Lace as shown in the illustration.

As mentioned in an earlier paragraph, the straight leg pants are a standard for the entire family of pants. You can widen your pant legs from the bell bottoms to the hostess palazzos by inserting godets. Fig. IV-6.3 illustrates how to cut and insert godets into the outside side seams to make bell bottoms. The drawings are self-explanatory.

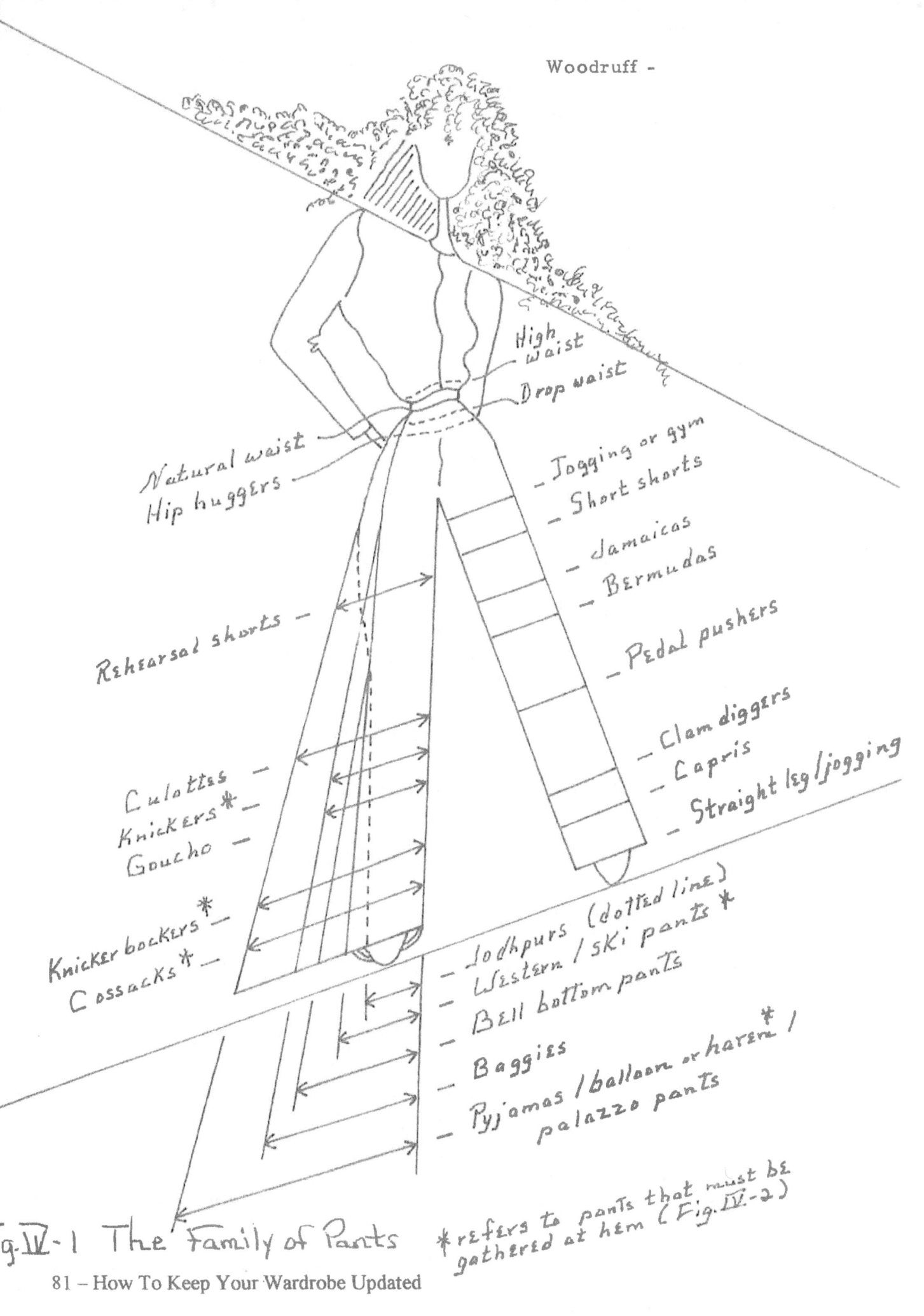

Woodruff –

High waist

Drop waist

Natural waist
Hip huggers

Jogging or gym
Short shorts

Jamaicas
Bermudas

Pedal pushers

Rehearsal shorts

Clam diggers
Capris
Straight leg/jogging

Culottes
Knickers *
Goucho

Knickerbockers *
Cossacks *

Jodhpurs (dotted line)
Western/ski pants *
Bell bottom pants

Baggies

Pyjamas/balloon or harem/
palazzo pants

g. IV-1 The Family of Pants

* refers to pants that must be gathered at hem (Fig. IV-2)

Fig. IV-2- Gathered Pant Hems

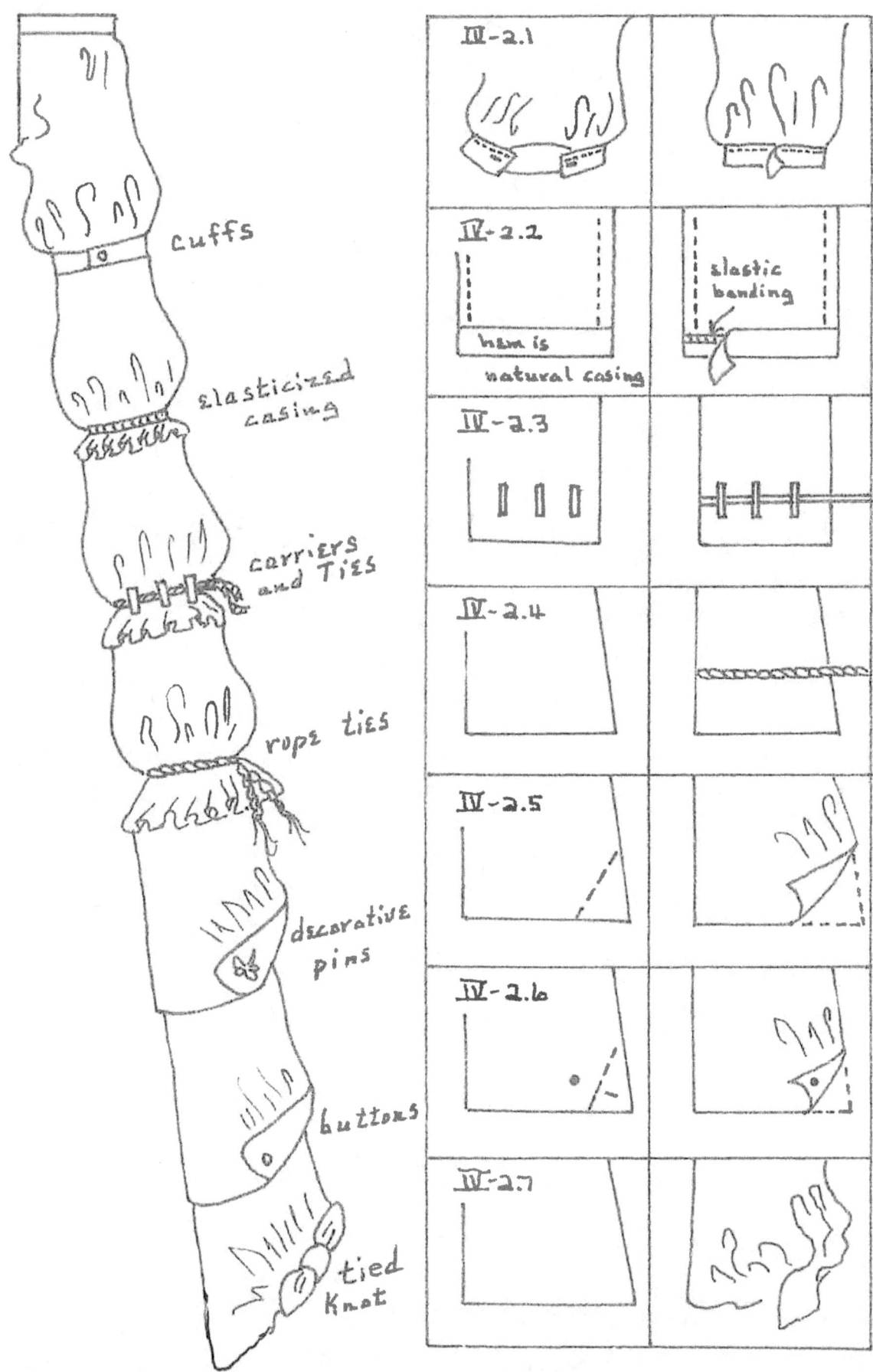

- cuffs
- elasticized casing
- carriers and Ties
- rope ties
- decorative pins
- buttons
- tied Knot

IV-2.1

IV-2.2 — ham is natural casing — elastic banding

IV-2.3

IV-2.4

IV-2.5

IV-2.6

IV-2.7

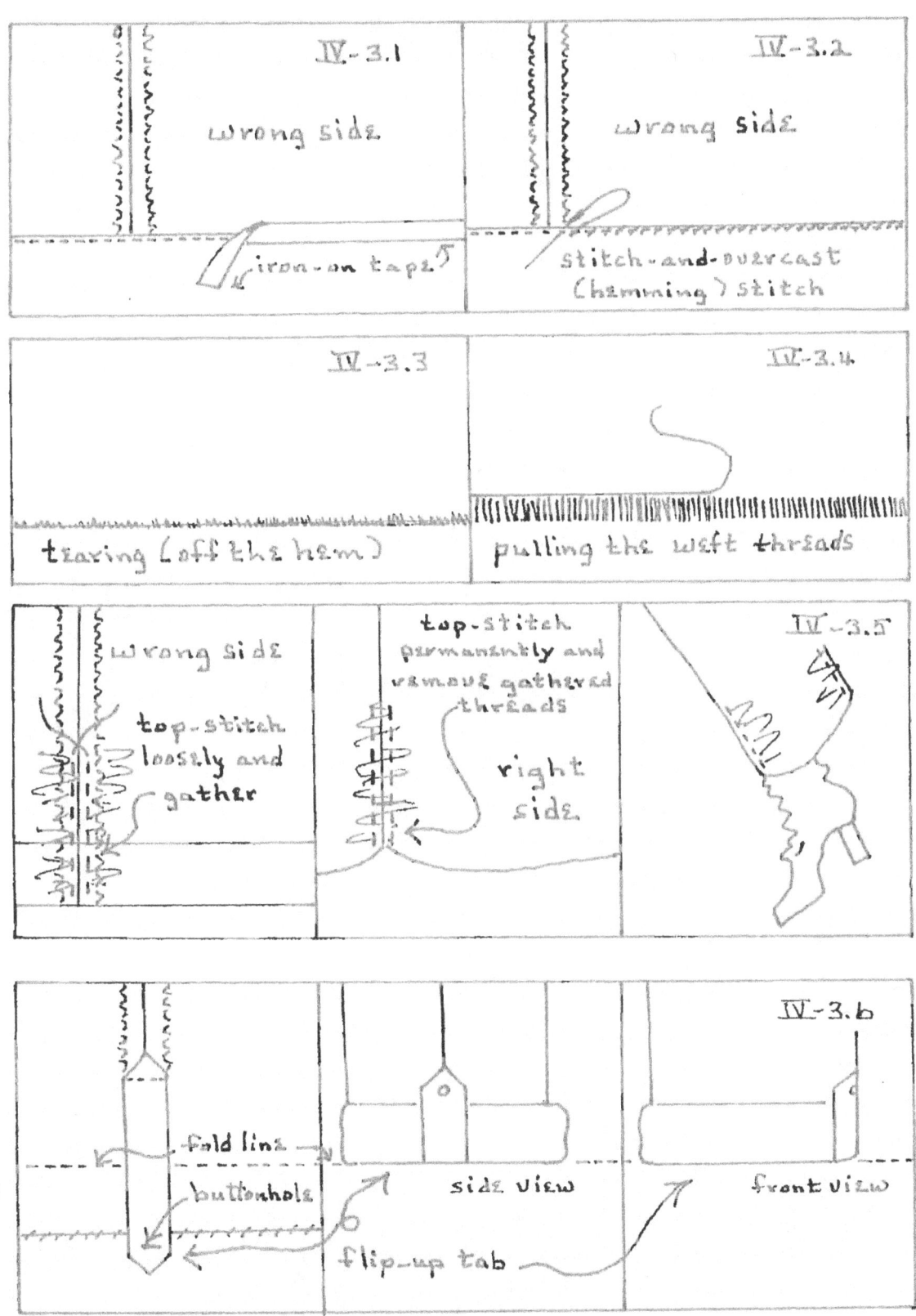

Fig. IV-3. Shortening Pants

Fig. IV-4 - Lengthening Pants   Woodruff -

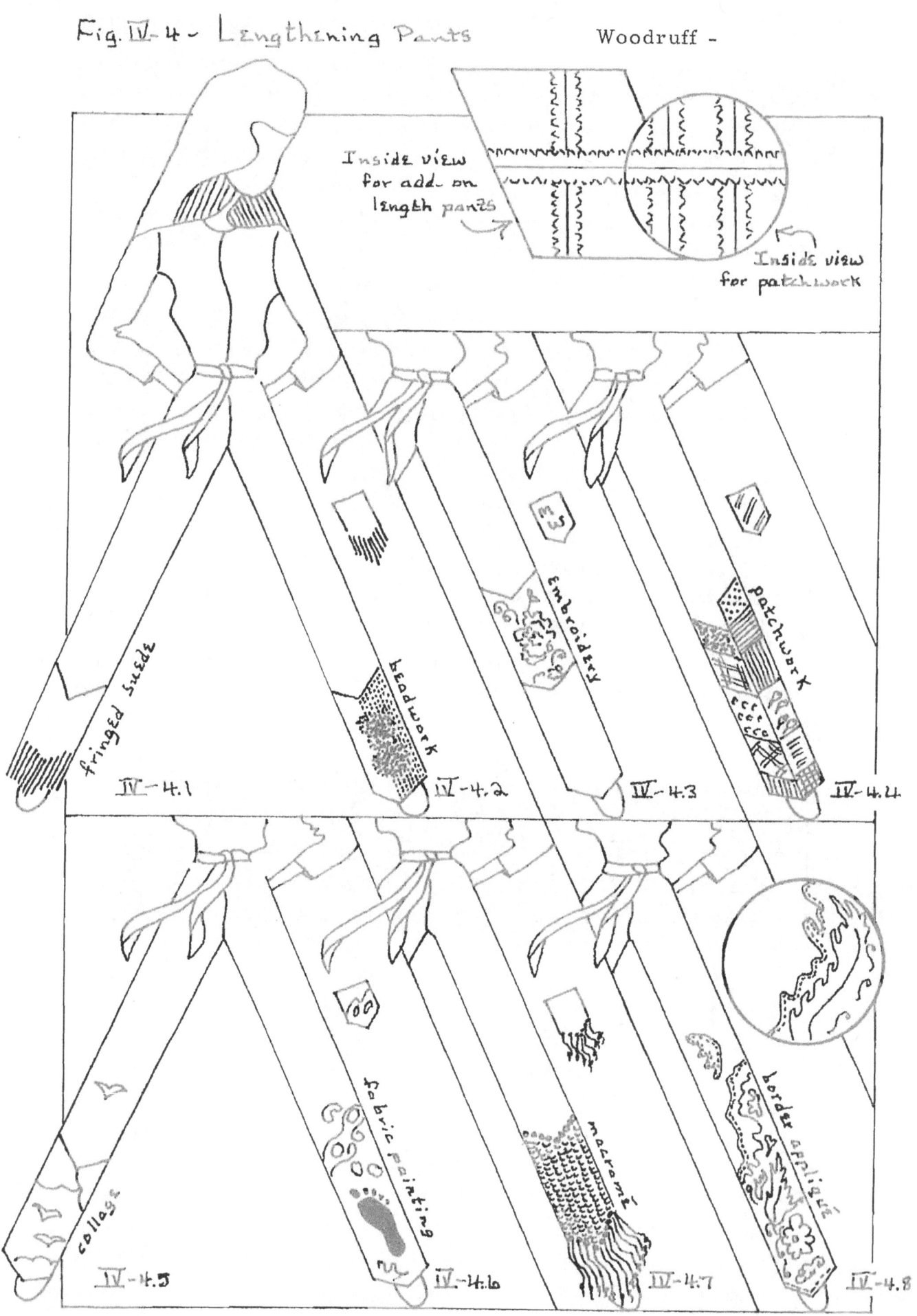

Inside view for add-on length pants

Inside view for patchwork

fringed suede   IV-4.1

beadwork   IV-4.2

Embroidery   IV-4.3

patchwork   IV-4.4

collage   IV-4.5

fabric painting   IV-4.6

macramé   IV-4.7

border appliqué   IV-4.8

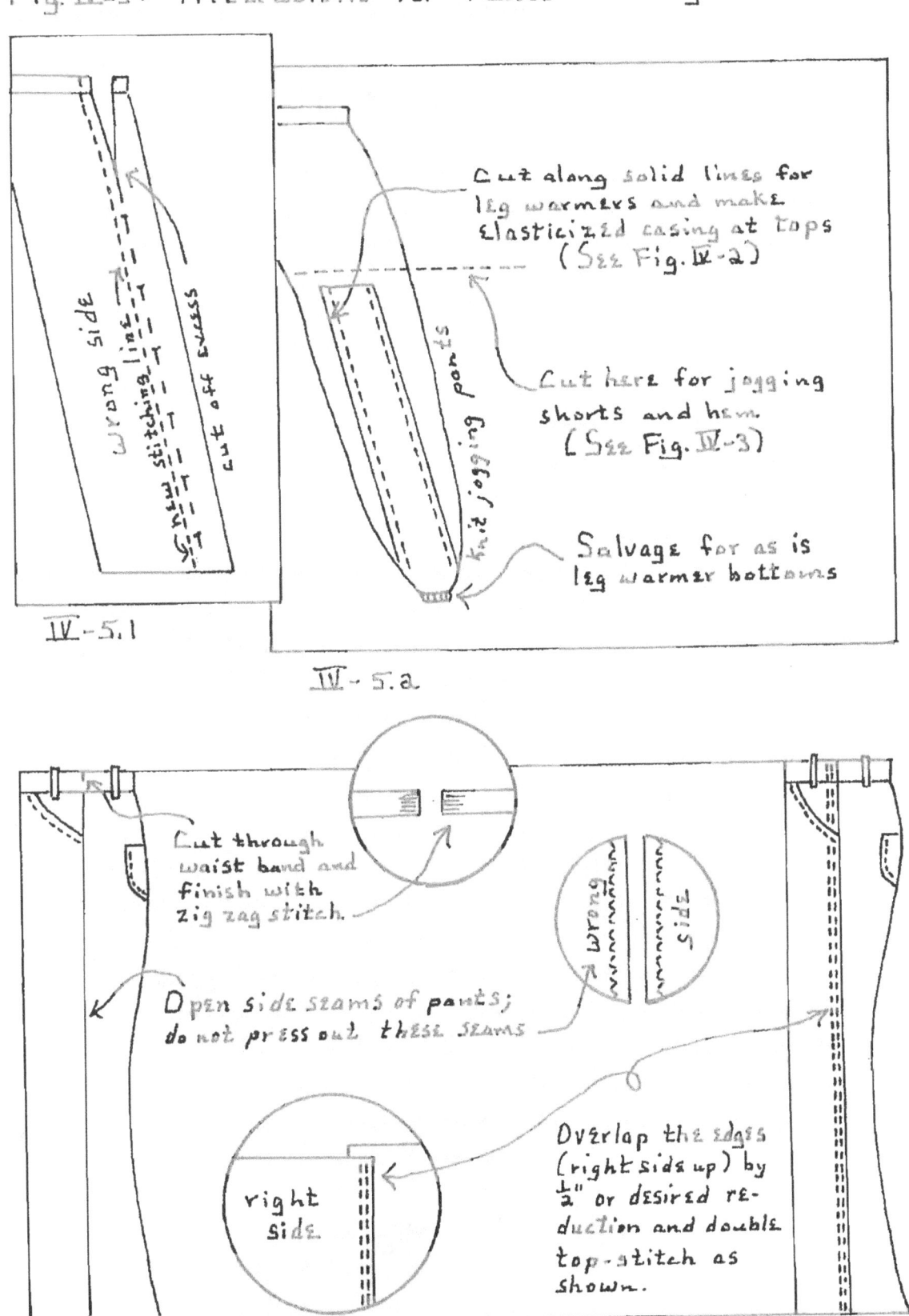

Fig. IV-5- Alterations for Pants Too Big

Cut along solid lines for
leg warmers and make
elasticized casing at tops
(See Fig. IV-2)

Cut here for jogging
shorts and hem.
[See Fig. IV-3]

Salvage for as is
leg warmer bottoms

wrong side

stitching line

cut off excess

knit jogging pants

IV-5.1

IV-5.2

Cut through
waist band and
finish with
zig zag stitch.

wrong side

side

Open side seams of pants;
do not press out these seams

right
side

Overlap the edges
(right side up) by
$\frac{1}{2}$" or desired re-
duction and double
top-stitch as
shown.

IV-5.3

Fig. IV-6 - Alterations for Pants Too Tight

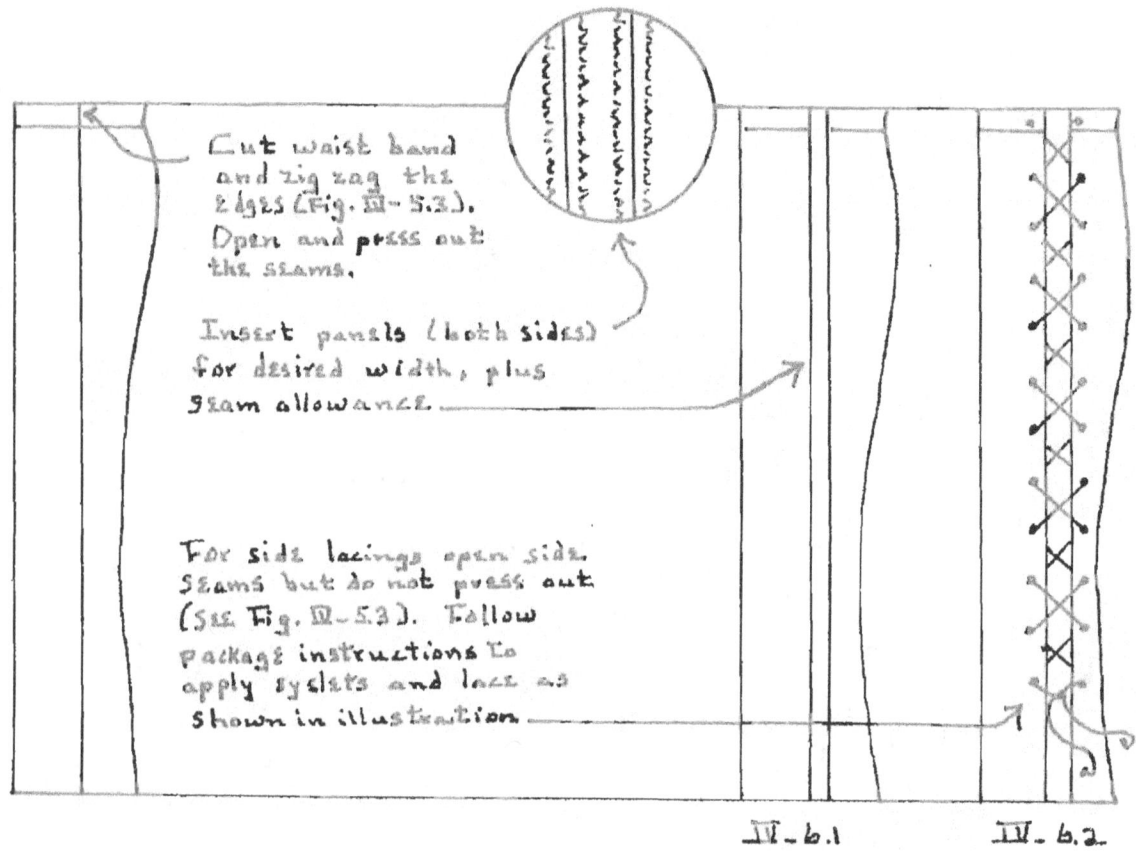

Cut waist band
and zig zag the
edges (Fig. IV-5.3).
Open and press out
the seams.

Insert panels (both sides)
for desired width, plus
seam allowance.

For side lacings open side
seams but do not press out
(see Fig. IV-53). Follow
package instructions to
apply eyelets and lace as
shown in illustration.

IV-6.1   IV-6.2

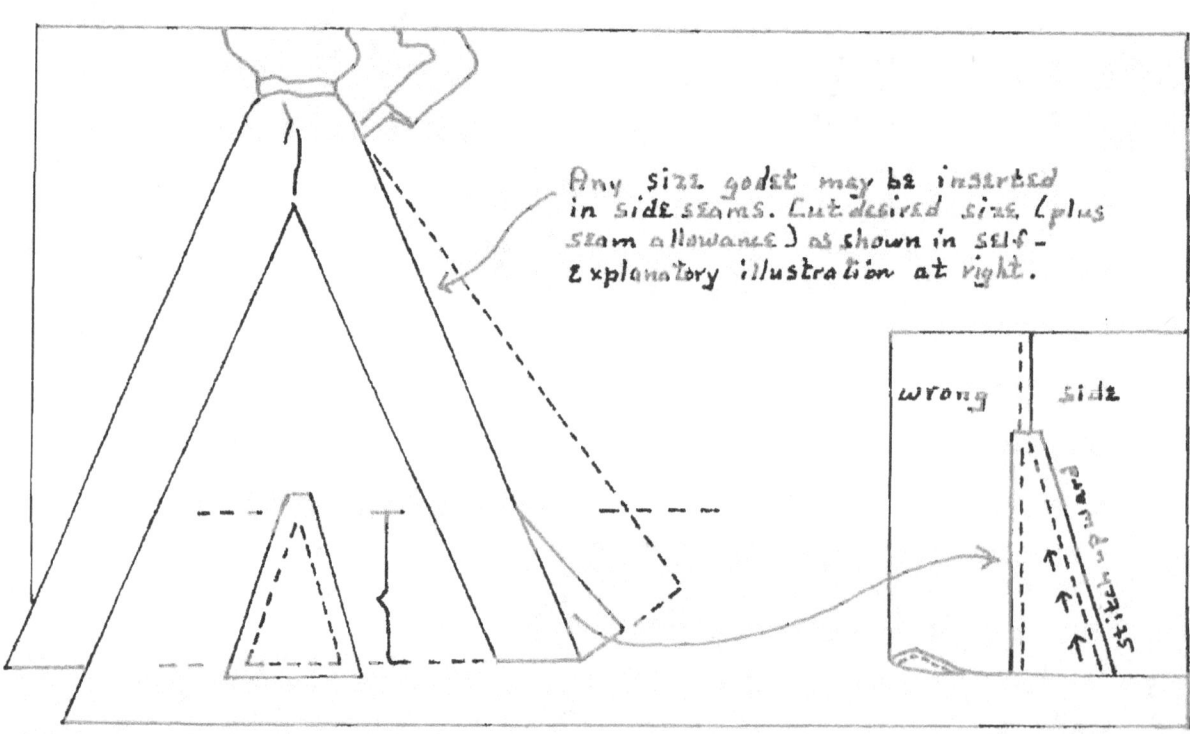

Any size godet may be inserted
in side seams. Cut desired size (plus
seam allowance) as shown in self-
explanatory illustration at right.

wrong   side

IV-6.3

Chapter V

The Family of Skirts

For many decades skirt lengths changed yearly. This was a highly lucrative phenomenon for all the people associated with the fashion arts and fashion merchandising. However, for the consumer such mercurial skirt length changes required much shopping and alterations time, and a great deal of money. Consequently women rebelled. Today any skirt length is acceptable because women make their own fashion choices. This chapter is a guide for those readers who, by their own choice, wish to change their skirt lengths, for whatever reason. Illustration V-1 represents the different skirt lengths. I believe that any of the lengths from the just below the knee length to the midi length will remain the classic length for street wear for many, many years. The maxi and floor lengths will undoubtedly continue to remain the classic lengths for formal and evening wear.

1.   Shortening Skirts at the Hemline

Fig. V-2 illustrates four simple ways to shorten skirts at the hemline. As with pants, the simplest way to shorten a skirt is to cut off the excess length and then hem, using either iron-on tape or the stitch-and-overcast hemming procedure (Fig. V-2.1 for straight or dirndl skirts and Fig. V-2.2 for flared and gored skirts). See Fig. IV-3.2 on how to work the stitch-and-overcast stitch.

If you would like to give your skirt a tailored, designer look, Fig. V-2.3 shows how to overlap and top-stitch for shortening skirts. This method looks especially effective with two or more overlapped rows on medium-weight fabrics, such as cottons and linens. Each overlapped row will shorten your skirt by 1/2" (see Fig. V-2.4). If you need to shorten your skirt by say two inches, make four overlapped rows. The top-stitching may be in either matching or contrasting thread. If you are the avant-garde type, consider using different colored thread for each row of top-stitching.

The underlap method (Fig. V-2.5) is somewhat the reverse of the overlap procedure. Use this method if you can use trim on the right side of your garment to cover the seam work. Unlike the overlap method, you can underlap more than 1/2" if you do not want multiple rows of trim on your skirt.

The last shortening method (Fig. V-2.6) works well on long, formal skirts of light-weight fabrics. You can shorten your skirt only a few inches using this method, which is really more desirable for design effect than practicality. This method is also favorable for prairie skirts if you have petticoats or underskirts to show.

2.   Shortening Skirts at the Waist

Shortening skirts at the waist (Fig. V-3) is usually more complicated than any of the previously mentioned methods because of the need to remove and resew the waistband and the zipper. For a very full skirt of delicate fabric, it may be more feasible to shorten the skirt at the waist. Remove the waistband and the zipper. Cut away the excess length at the top-- be sure to allow for seam allowances (Fig. V-3.1). Working on the wrong side, cut away the excess fabric and stitch as illustrated (Fig. V-3.2).

Optional alternative to Fig. V-3.2: consider gathering the waist of the skirt to fit the waistband. Readjust the zipper and resew the waist to the waistband (Fig. V-3.3).

3.   Letting Hems Down

The most logical way to lengthen a skirt is simply to let down the hem (Fig. V-4.1). However, if there is not enough material for the required hem, you may want to make a hem facing (Fig. V-4.2). This would be necessary for skirts of medium to heavy-weight fabrics. Commercially-made lace hem facing, which usually comes in 1-3/4" widths, works especially well because the lace gives your skirt the appearance of a lace underslip. For circular skirts and those of delicate fabrics a very small hem (3/4" or less) would be preferable to a big hem and would need no facing.

If you do not want a hem facing or do not have sufficient fabric for one, consider a natural fringe hem (Fig. V-4.3). Let the hem all the way down and pull the weft, or width-wise, threads (Fig. IV-3.4). This method works well only with coarse or loosely woven fabrics, such as some of the wools and cottons. If you like the Western, prairie, pioneer, or Bohemian look, consider the natural fringe hem for your skirt.

4.   Lengthening Dirndl Skirts

A dirndl skirt is either tubular or very full, of straight-grain fabric, with the top gathered to fit the waistband. Fig. V-5 illustrates how to lengthen a dirndl skirt if you do not have sufficient hem allowance for your desired length. The lengthening inserts, or bands, should be cut on straight grain of fabric, the same as the dirndl skirt. Choose equal weight fabrics in complementary or contrasting colors for the lengthening inserts. The fabrics may be in contrasting textures, such as light-weight cotton chintz with light-weight cotton seersucker, or in contrasting prints, such as medium-weight cotton gingham with medium-weight cotton calico. The stretch, or give, of your fabric, if any, should run horizontally with the body. Always allow extra yardage to repeat the fabric of the insert elsewhere--self belt, scarf, top, cuffs--for the balanced, designer look.

5.   Lengthening Flared and Gored Skirts

Flared and gored skirts (Fig. V-6) can be lengthened with inserts, or bands, in the same manner as dirndl skirts, except that the inserts must be cut on a bias (Fig. V-6.1) and the sides of the skirt must be re-cut slightly (Fig. V-6.2 and Fig. V-6.3) in order to accommodate the lengthening insert. Inserts for gored skirts cut on a bias should be cut consistent with the straight of grain of the gores (Fig. V-6.5).

6.   Lengthening Skirts with Leathers

Lengthening skirts with leather borders (Fig. V-7) is far easier to do than it may look. Leather borders can be used on skirts of leather, suede, and heavy-weight fabrics.

For Fig. V-7.1, apply grommets as illustrated and lace your border to the skirt as you would lace your shoes. Grommets (or eyelets) are avaible at yardage stores and hobby houses, and come complete with the necessary installation equipment and instructions.

Fig. V-7.2 is simply a leather border sewn to the hem of the skirt. The fringes are cut approximately 3/8" to 1/4" wide, as shown. Com-mercially-made fringed borders are also available in leather and suede in a variety of widths, weights, and colors. For medium to heavy-weight leathers and suedes it may be necessary for you to have your borders sewn on by a tailor or a furrier. Bear in mind the drycleaning expense of a leather-bordered skirt before you undertake this project.

Fig. V-7.3 illustrates a leather border with leather or suede collage work of different colors. The creative possibilities using this technique are boundless for unique, one-of-a-kind artforms that you can wear. Use leather-on-leather glue, available at leather and fur workshops, for the collage project.

7.   Lengthening Skirts with Furs and Feathers

Furs and feathers are another way of lengthening your skirts, and very elegantly at that (Fig. V-8).

For a fur border (V-8.1) salvage pieces of fur from old clothing. Cut into desired width and join the fur pieces together using the overcast stitch, as shown in Fig. V-8.2. Use an upholstery needle and wax thread. On the fur side, if any furs get caught in the overcasting, pick them out with your needle. Attach the fur border to the skirt hem using the running stitch, as shown in Fig. V-8.3. When your work is completed, check the right side if any furs got caught in the stitching. For drycleaning, consider detaching the fur border to save cleaning costs.

Fig. V-8.4 illustrates an elegant feather border as a means to lengthening a skirt. Feather hem borders should be used only with very fine, delicate fabrics, such as silk chiffon or taffeta. Secure the feathers to the border (of equal weight fabric as the skirt) by using two or three overcast stitches over the shaft of each feather (Fig. V-8.5). Using a fine needle and thread, work from the bottom row up to the top (Fig. V-8.6). For the top few rows, work the tips of the shafts downward underneath the feathers of the preceding row, as indicated in the V-8.4 illustration. Secure the feather border to the hem of the skirt using the running stitch, the same procedure as for the fur border (Fig. V-8.3). When your skirt needs drycleaning, detach the feather border, unless you are not concerned with excessive cleaning expenses.

Another feather border you might care to consider is marabou, commercially-assembled, fur-like trimming made of soft, downy feathers, that comes in a variety of widths and colors.

8. Lengthening Skirts with Decorative Trims and Craftsworks

Using decorative trims and craftsworks to lengthen your skirts can be anything from commercially-made trims to your own artworks. Also, refer to Fig. IV-4, Lengthening Pants, for even further creative means to lengthening your skirts by incorporating your artistic talents. Fig. V-9 and Fig. IV-4 are illustrated to serve as an impetus for you to create your own artforms that you can wear. Now you really can wear your "Picasso" to the Riviera!

Commercially-made fringe (Fig. V-9.1) is a very simple way to lengthen your skirt. There is a wide range of different types of fringes available in several different widths. Attach the fringe to the skirt by using the running stitch or the overcast stitch by hand, or top-stitch by machine.

For a romantic or nostalgic look, consider lace or pleat trim (Fig. V-9.2) to lengthen your skirts of delicate-weight fabric. Again, there is a vast market of laces in a myriad of colors, textures, and widths. Heat-set pleat trims (in man-made fabrics) will not unset with washings.

The applique lengthening border (Fig. V-9.3) would enable you a one-of-a-kind work of art. Sew on a solid colored border of desired length and then hem (see Fig. V-5.3). Cut out designs from printed fabrics of equal weight--be sure to allow 1/4" allowance around the design. Tuck under this 1/4" allowance and secure to the border using tiny running stitches or overcast stitches very close to the edge of the design. Or, you may use a printed border fabric for your lengthening border. Then cut out a design(s) already in the border print, incorporate this design piece into the border, and extend it partially onto the skirt itself for the designer, border print look, as illustrated in Fig. V-9.3.

Whether you like the romantic, nostalgic, or prairie look, commercially-made ruffles are a very easy way to lengthen your skirt (Fig. V-9.4). Try to match the fabric weight of the ruffles to the fabric weight of the skirt. If you have extra fabric to match the skirt, it is very easy to make your own ruffles (see detail insert for Fig. V-9.4). The ruffle width should be one and one-half times the circumference of the skirt. Make allowance for hemming, gathering, and seam stitching.

Macramé as a lengthening border (Fig. V-9.5) will give your skirt a very expressive, designer look. If you are unfamiliar with making macramé, there are volumes of literature on the craft at the public libraries. Macramé is very simple to make from most illustrated instructions. Macramé borders team best with leathers, suedes, or course wools or mohairs. You will probably need to make your border in several pieces and then join the pieces together. And do make the border detachable to save on drycleaning costs of your skirt. Also, make a macramé rope-style belt for the coordinated, designer look.

If you like Americana, a patchwork border (Fig. V-9.6) might be your choice for a lengthening border. Try to keep the weight of the fabric for the patchwork and the skirt itself as consistent as possible. See detail insert for Fig. IV-4.4 on how to join the patchwork. You can repeat a few pieces of patchwork elsewhere on your skirt and even make a patchwork pocket and/or self belt.

9. Lengthening Skirts with Handkerchieves

If you are the bold type who likes exotic clothes, try using hand-kerchieves (Fig. V-10) for lengthening a skirt. You can use commercially-made squares or make your own with self-fringe edges. Pull the warp (lengthwise) and weft (width-wise) threads until you have an approximately 1/8" natural fringe.

Fig. V-10.2 through V-10.4 are self-explanatory on how to attach the squares to the hem. A matching handkerchief top (Fig. V-10.1) would be an exciting complement to this type of skirt.

For a shorter skirt, say knee length, you could make the entire skirt using large squares. A handkerchief skirt is a good investment because of its versatility; it works for casual as well as formal occasions.

10. Special Alterations

(a) Alterations for Skirts Too Big

The traditional method of making alterations for a skirt too big is simply to take it in at the sides, as shown in the self-explanatory illustration in Fig. V-11.1, which shows the model wearing her skirt inside out.

Fig. V-11.2 and Fig. V-11.3 are alternative methods to reducing the width of your skirt. Open a seam, side or front, and cut through the waistband. Do not press out the seams--leave them as shown in Fig. V-11.5. Finish the cut waistband edges with machine zig-zagging to prevent raveling (Fig. V-11.4). Working on the right side of the skirt, overlap one edge over the other (Fig. V-11.6 and Fig. V-11.7 for Fig. V-11.2 and Fig. V-11.3 respectively) and secure the edges by using either buttons or pins (Fig. V-11.2) or one or two rows of tailored-look top-stitching (Fig. V-11.3). The skirt in Fig. V-11.2 can be worn either as a solo skirt fully buttoned or as an overskirt partially unbuttoned with longer, ruffled skirts for the prairie look.

(b) Alterations for Skirts Too Tight

Fig. V-12 illustrates what you can do to make minimal width alterations to your skirt. Fig. V-12.1 incorporates the use of grommets for skirts of leathers, wools, or heavy-weight cottons. Open but do not press out the seams (Fig. V-12.4) so that you can use these seams as an anchor for your grommets. Cut through the waistband and finish off the edges with machine zig-zagging to prevent raveling (Fig. V-12.3). Grommets are available at yardage stores and hobby houses, and come complete with installation tools and instructions. Use macramé thread or yarn for the lacings. This type of skirt can be worn as an overskirt by lacing the skirt opening only, say, one-third of the way down.

If you need up to two inches to let out, Fig. V-12.2 may be your answer. Do not make the side bands more than one inch wide (excluding seam allowance). The band should be in a fabric of weight equal to the skirt, in a contrasting or complementary color. Leather or suede bands would be ideal for wool skirts. For woven fabric bands, the stretch, or give, of the fabric should run width-wise with the body.

Woodruff –

micro-mini

mini

just above the knee

just below the knee

midi

maxi

floor length

Fig.Ⅴ-1 The Skirt Lengths

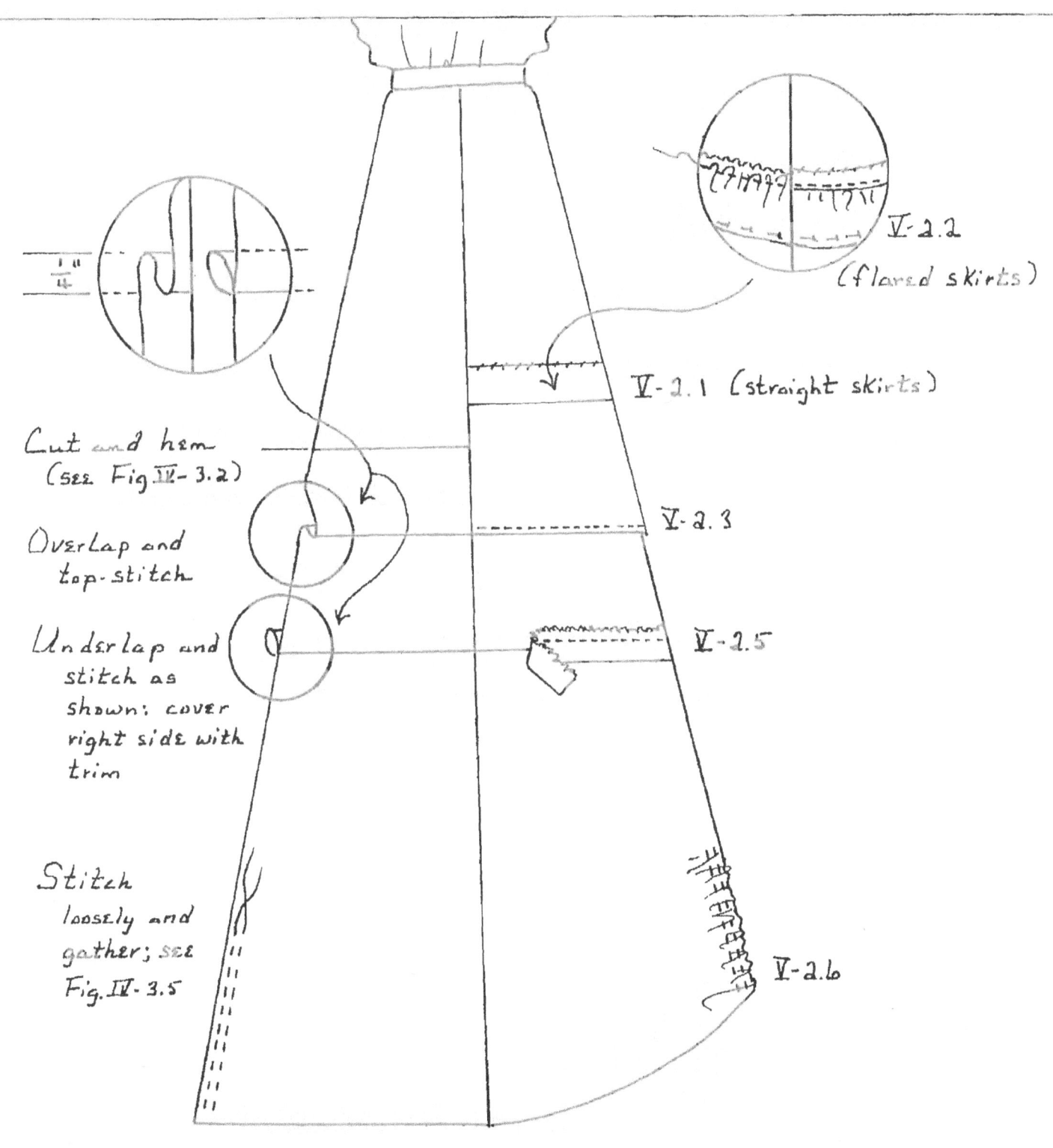

V-2.2
(flared skirts)

V-2.1 (straight skirts)

Cut and hem
(see Fig. IV-3.2)

Overlap and
top-stitch

V-2.3

Underlap and
stitch as
shown: cover
right side with
trim

V-2.5

Stitch
loosely and
gather; see
Fig. IV-3.5

V-2.6

¼"

Fig V-2 - Shortening Skirts at the Hem

Fig. Ⅴ·3 – Shortening Skirts at the Waist
(for skirts too delicate to shorten at the hemline)

Cut away excess here
(both sides)

Cut

wrong side

Ⅴ-3.1

Ⅴ-3.2

Ⅴ-3.3

3.1 – Cut away desired length;
   remove waistband and zipper.

3.2 – Cut away excess fabric at both sides
   to adjust to waistband, as shown in illustration.

3.3 – Sew side seams as shown in 3.2; readjust zipper accordingly;
   fit and resew waist to waistband.

Fig. V-4 – Letting Hems Down

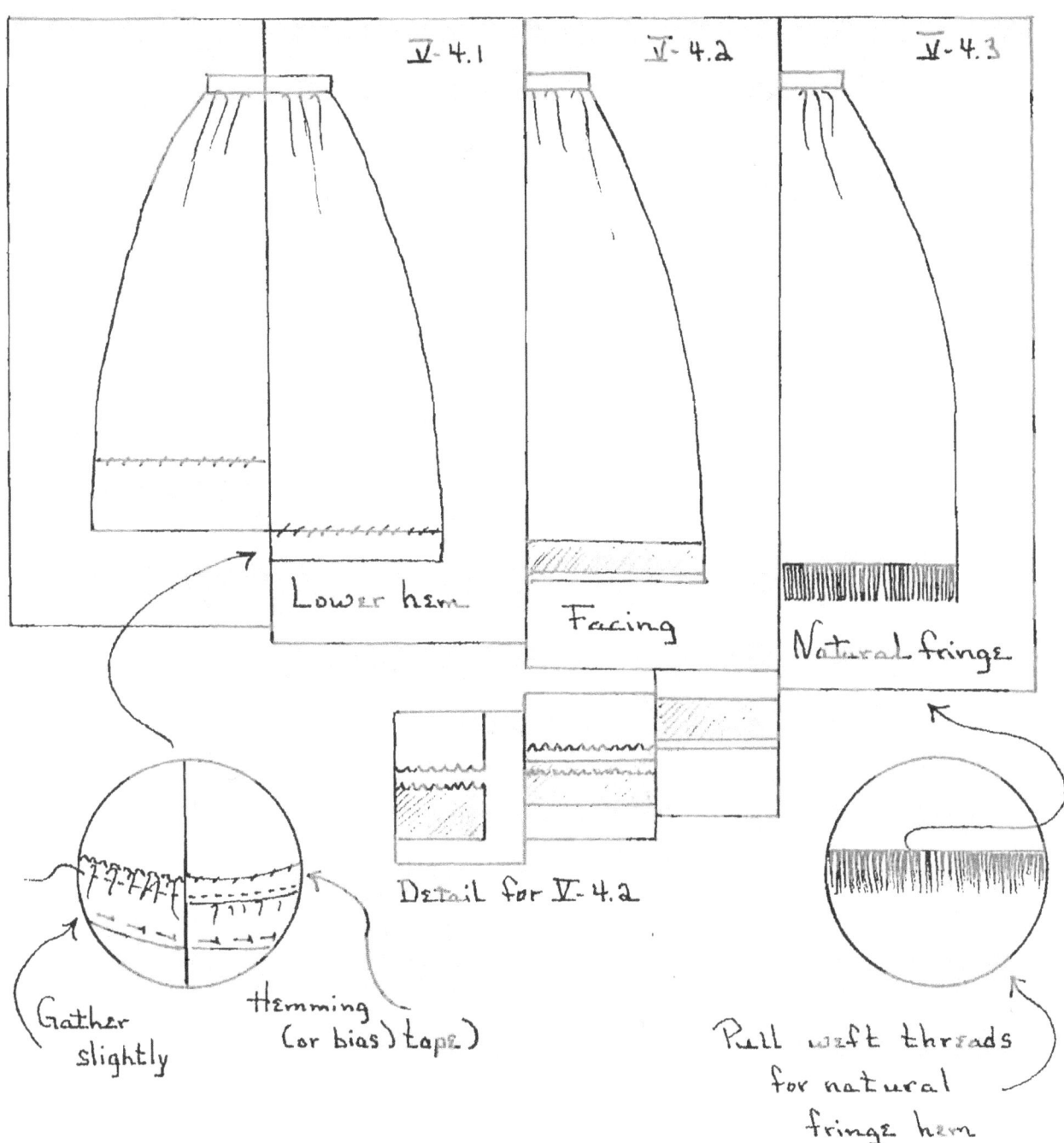

V-4.1

V-4.2

V-4.3

Lower hem

Facing

Natural fringe

Detail for V-4.2

Gather slightly

Hemming (or bias) tape)

Pull weft threads for natural fringe hem

Fig. V-5 - Lengthening Dirndl Skirts*

* A dirndl skirt is tubular, or full, of straight-grain fabric, with the top gathered to fit the waistband.

Fig. V-6 – Lengthening Flared and Gored Skirts

V-6.1 – Illustration shows how to cut lengthening panels on a bias.

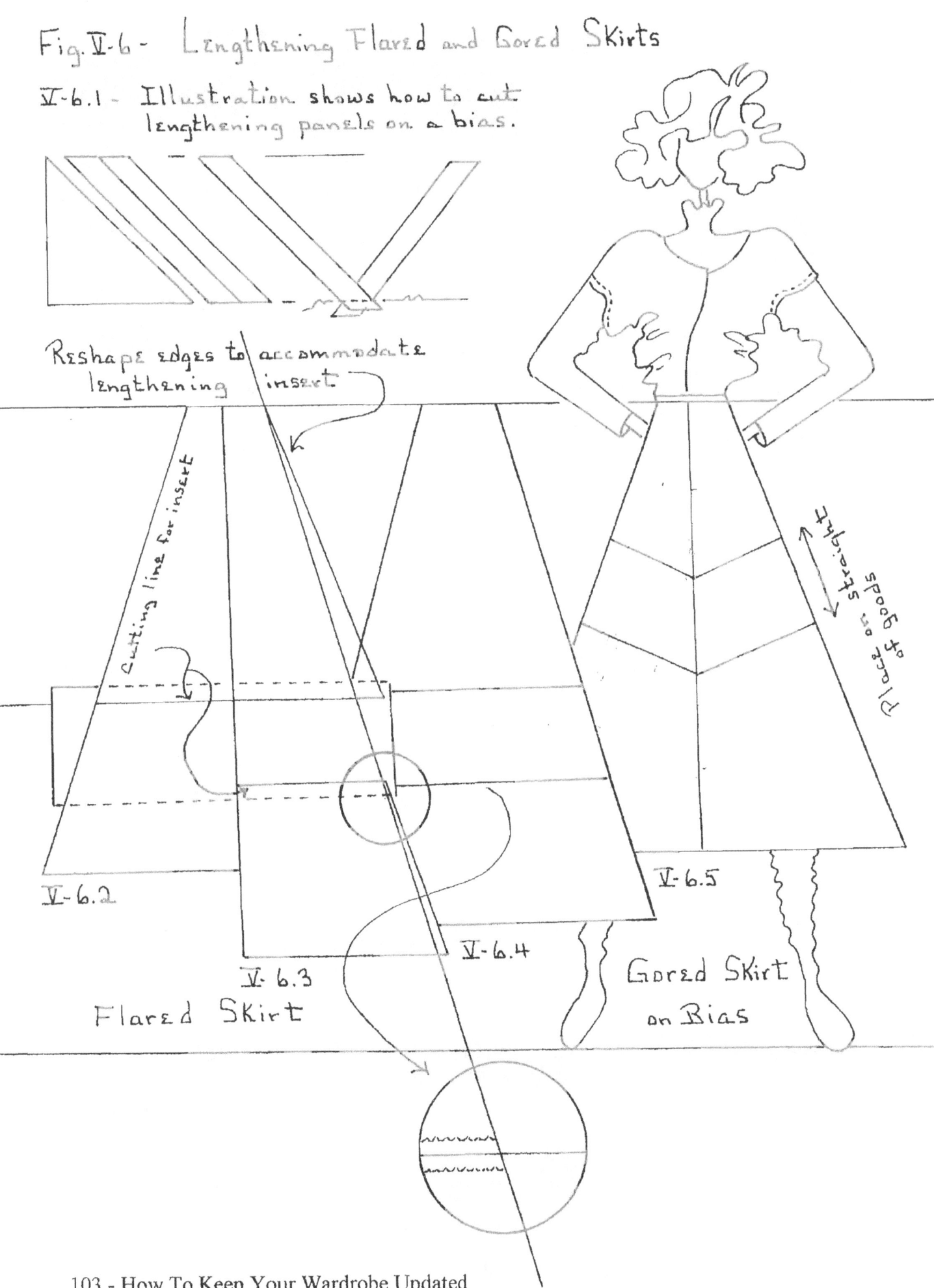

Reshape edges to accommodate lengthening insert.

Cutting line for insert

V-6.2

V-6.3

V-6.4

Flared Skirt

V-6.5

Gored Skirt on Bias

Place on straight of goods

Fig. V-7- Lengthening Skirts with Leathers

Woodruff -

V-7.1

V-7.2

V-7.3

Fig. V-8- Lengthening Skirts with Fur and Feathers

V-8.2- Join fur pieces using overcast stitching

V-8.3- Use running stitch to secure fur border to skirt

V-8.5- Secure feathers to border using overcast stitch over shaft of each feather

V-8.6- Use fine needle and thread and work from bottom to top

Fig. V-9. *Lengthening Skirts with Decorative Trims and Craftsworks

Commercially-made fringe

V-9.1

Lace or pleat trim

V-9.2

Appliqué border (see Fig. IV-4.8)

V-9.3

Ruffle trim

V-9.4

Macramé (see Fig. IV-4.7)

V-9.5

Patchwork (see Fig. IV-4.4)

V-9.6

*See also Fig. IV-4

Fig. V-10 - Lengthening Skirts with Handkerchieves*

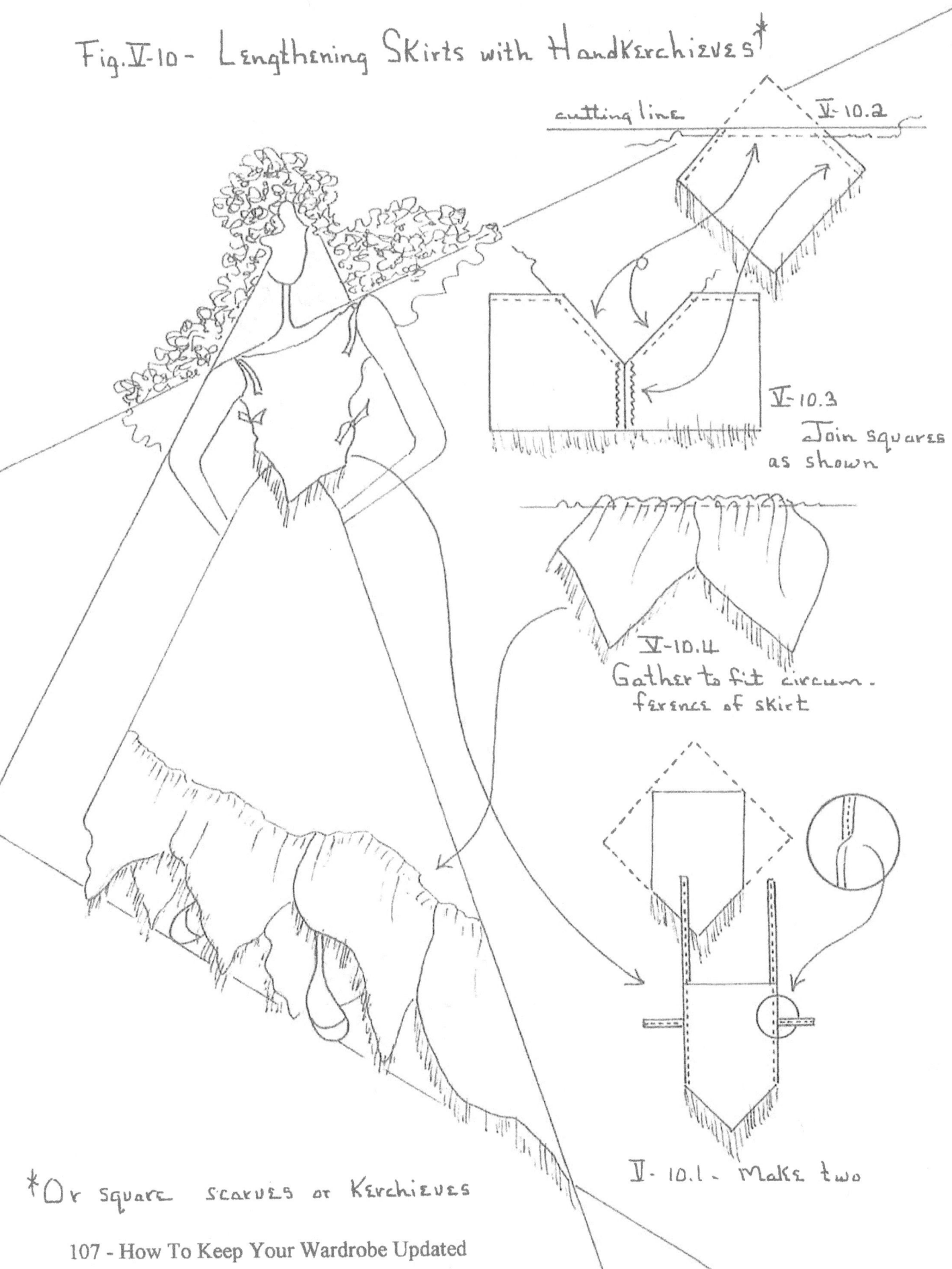

cutting line V-10.2

V-10.3
Join squares
as shown

V-10.4
Gather to fit circum-
ference of skirt

V-10.1 - Make two

*Or square scarves or kerchieves

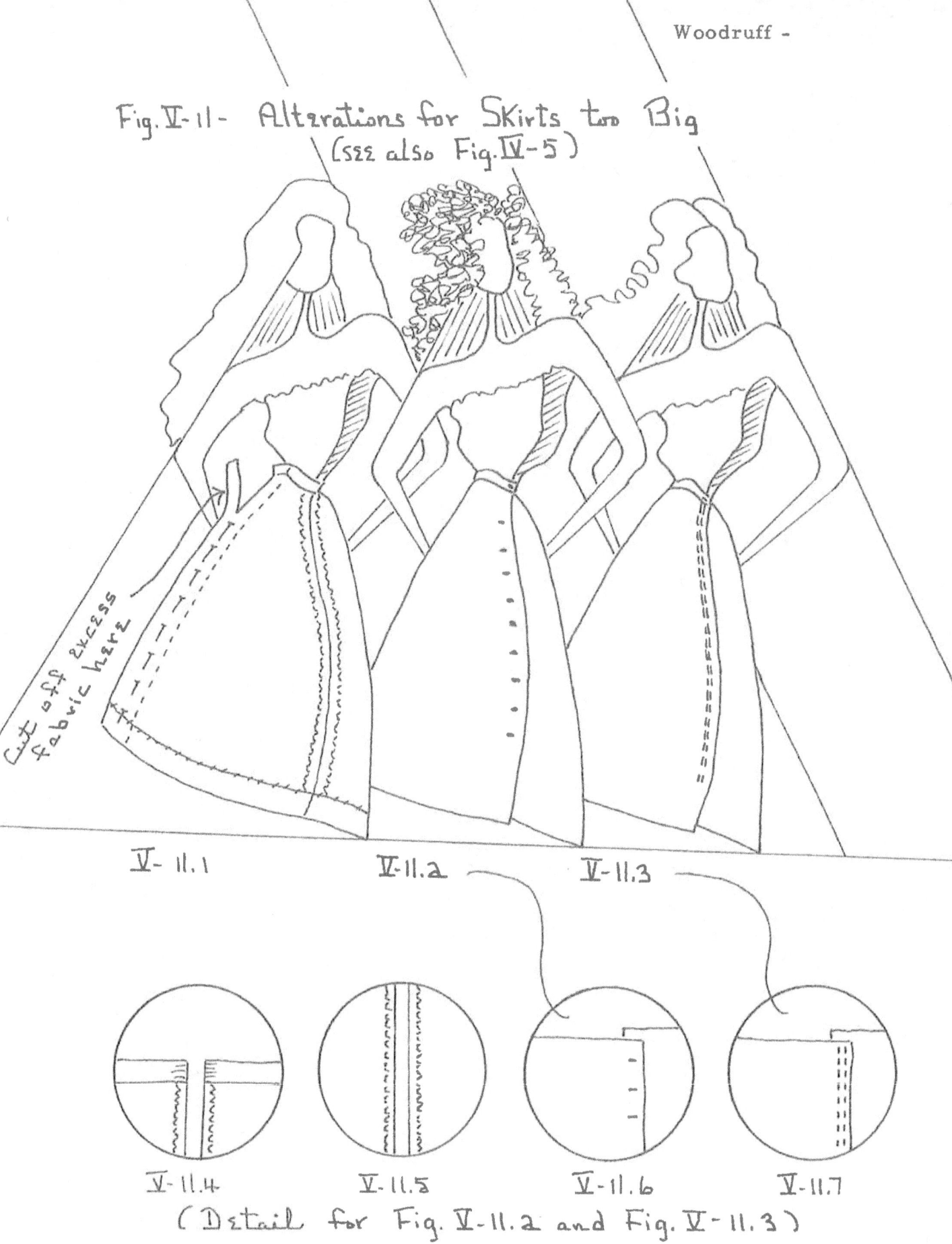

Fig. V-11- Alterations for Skirts too Big
(see also Fig. IV-5)

Cut off excess fabric here

V- 11.1   V-11.2   V-11.3

V-11.4   V-11.5   V-11.6   V-11.7

(Detail for Fig. V-11.2 and Fig. V-11.3)

Fig. V-12- Alterations for Skirts too Tight
(see also Fig. IV-6)

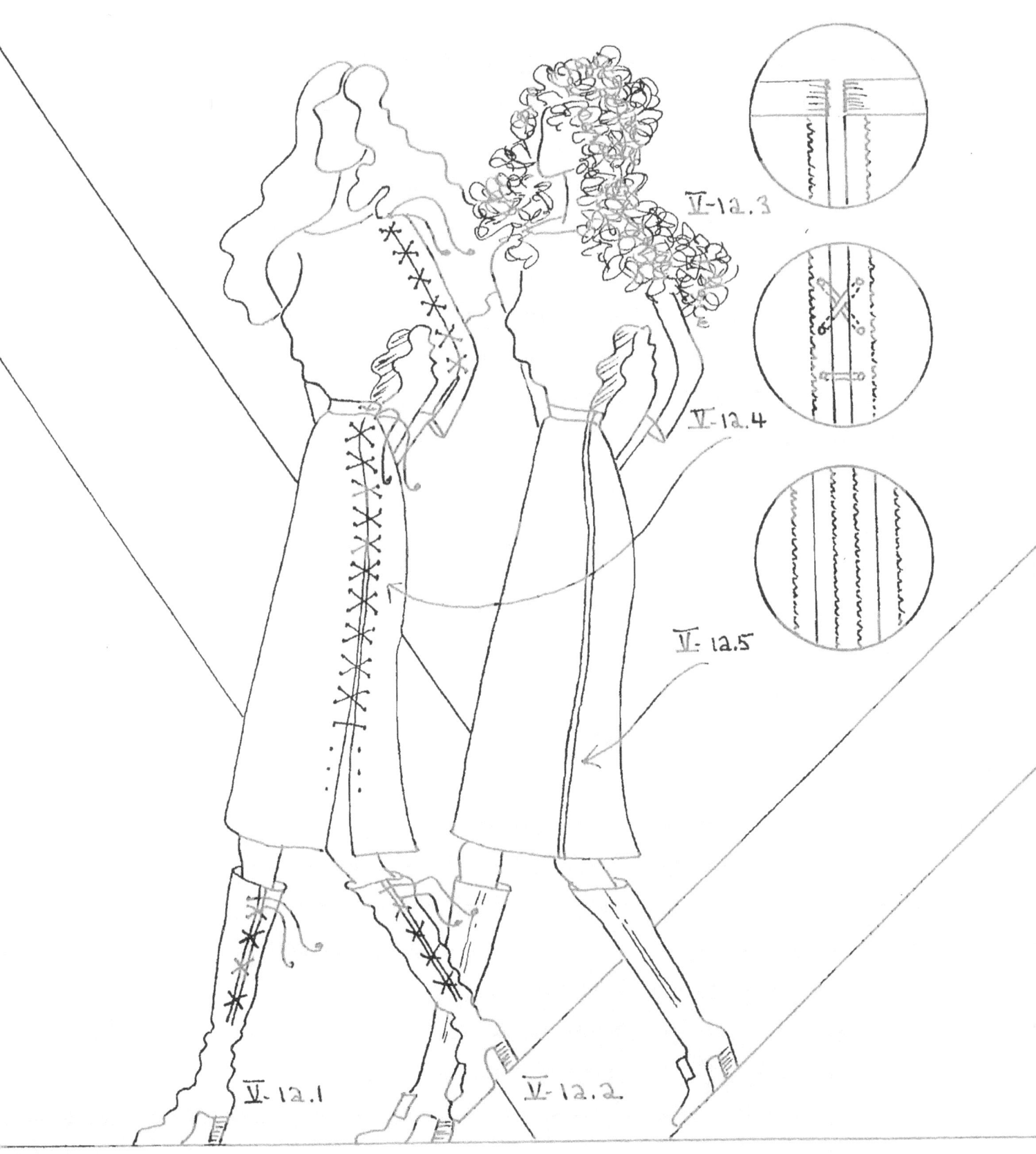

V-12.3

V-12.4

V-12.5

V-12.1   V-12.2

Chapter VI

Dresses and Their Variations

1.   Waisted Dresses

(a) Make Peplum Top and Skirt from Dress Too Long or Too Short

Aside from the myriad of methods of altering the skirt lengths

(see Chapter V - The Family of Skirts), the waisted dress presents yet

another exciting challenge to altering the dress too long or too short.

Fig. VI-1 illustrates how you can make a peplum top from a dress of

an undesirable length.

For a dress with a skirt gathered at the waist, cut a short skirt

(peplum) 6" to 12" (plus hem allowance) below the waistline (Fig. VI-1.1)

and hem (Fig. VI-1.2). See Fig. IV-3.1 and Fig. IV-3.2 for hemming

instructions.

For a dress without a full skirt, cut a tunic 10" to 18" (plus hem

allowance) below the waistline (see Fig. VI-6) and wear with either a longer skirt or pants. However, please note that if your dress is any length above the knee and you no longer wish to wear short skirts, simply wear the dress as is tunic style and team it with a belt and either a longer skirt or pants. The peplum top, with or without its matching skirt, can be worn with most of your skirts and pants, and add versatility to your wardrobe.

If the skirt is originally too long, you may have enough material for a shorter skirt to match your new peplum top (Fig. VI-1.2). On the other hand, if the original skirt is too short and you do not want a tunic, you may be able to salvage enough material to make a short athletic skirt for tennis, golf, or skating (Fig. VI-1.3).

(b) Add a Tier or Border to Dress Too Short

Fig. VI-2 shows four versions of lengthening a dress too short. Also refer to Chapter V - The Family of Skirts for additional ideas for lengthening your dress too short.

Fig. VI-2.1 is basically a long tunic worn over a longer skirt. Please note that the tiered skirt can be a slip with a contrasting or complementary border coming below your dress too short. For the designer look and balanced effect one sleeve is made in the same fabric and color as the tiered skirt or underskirt. Use the original sleeve as a pattern for the new sleeve. Or, you can remove both sleeves and use the sleeveless dress as a jumper to wear over light-knit dresses or with sweaters and skirts and pants.

Fig. VI-2.2 is simply a border added to your short skirt and is described in detail in Chapter V and illustrated in Fig. V-5 and Fig. V-6. Note the sash belt for the balanced, designer look.

Fig. VI-2.3 shows how to lengthen a dress by using an insert. Here part of the original dress skirt was used for the border to give the garment an overall balanced effect. The long sash belt can match either fabric.

If the skirt to be lengthened is flared or gored, refer to Fig. V-6 on how to cut and sew in the lengthening insert.

Another version of lengthening a skirt is illustrated in Fig. VI-2.4 by making a gathered ruffle border. Use commercially-made ruffles or refer to Fig. V-9.4 on how to make your own ruffles. For this dress the stole (matching the ruffle) gave the ensemble a pleasing coordinated look

(c) Make an Overskirt from Dress Too Long or Too Short

In recent years, the layered look has become very popular, making the overskirt an ideal item to wear for any number of casual and formal occasions.

In Fig. VI-3.1 the skirt is gathered up at one side using the flip-up tab sewn inside the skirt (VI-3.2), enabling you to wear the skirt up or down, with or without an underskirt. This method can also be used to shorten pants (Fig. IV-3.6).

A tunic top can be cut from a dress too short. Fig. VI-3.3 shows the diagonal cutting line for the formal look in Fig. VI-3.4. Make a long self belt to match either the overskirt or the underskirt. For a more casual look, the dress may be cut straight across instead of diagonally, and worn with a skirt of any length from below the knee to mid-calf (or midi).

(d) Widen a Dress Too Tight

If you have a dress that is still in excellent condition but too tight due to weight gain, consider side panel stripes for both pragmatic and decorative purposes. Let out the seams, the sleeves, and the sides, and sew in a contrasting stripe on each side as shown in Fig. VI-4.1. If your dress is say 1" too tight, cut two stripes (for each side of the dress) 1/2" wide (plus seam allowance).

If the dress is also too tight across the shoulders, remove the sleeves (Fig. VI-4.2). For the designer look, make each side panel stripe of two contrasting or complementary colors.

Another way to alleviate a dress too tight across the shoulders is to cut a diagonal, off-the-shoulder neckline, as shown in Fig. VI-4.3. The back zipper would have to be either readjusted or installed into the side panel stripe.

See also Chapter IV on page 00 - Alterations for Pants Too Tight, and Chapter V on page 00 - Alterations for Skirts Too Tight.

(e) Open Up a Dress Too Tight

Depending on the style and cut of the dress that is too tight, you may be able to salvage the garment simply by opening it up, as shown in Fig. VI-5.1. Note that just simply removing the sleeves and collar from a garment can do wonders for the dress that is too tight.

However, the style of the dress in Fig. VI-5.1 illustrates an almost idealistic solution to altering a too tight garment. Fig. VI-5.2 shows another method how you can easily make a bolero from the top of your dress, or a top, too tight. You will need to remove the back or side zipper and sew up the seam, remove the sleeves, cut open the front, and cut above the waistline as shown. The skirt can be cut open to be worn as an overskirt (Fig. VI-5.1). Or you can insert a front (or side) panel stripe to compensate for the additional necessary width, as shown in Fig. VI-5.2. Wherever you cut the old dress--down the front of the top for the bolero, for example--press an inside "hem" (seam) and finish as you would the hem of your skirt (see Fig. IV-3.1 and IV-3.2). If you need a facing, refer to Fig. V-4.2.

Both ensembles in Fig. VI-5 are more versatile than the original garments because they can be mixed and matched with other tops, skirts, and pants, and create a number of different outfits.

2.   Non-Waisted Dresses

(a) Make a Tunic Top from Dress Too Short

One of the easiest things you can do with a non-waisted dress too short is to turn it into a tunic--long or short--and wear it with your skirts and pants as you would any other overblouse. Whether you make a long or short tunic, you need not remove the sleeves and collar, if any. A non-waisted dress as long as knee length can be worn as a belted tunic with longer skirts or pants.

For shorter versions, simply cut the dress as shown in Fig. VI-6.1 and Fig. VI-6.2, and hem as you would a skirt (see Fig. IV-3.1 and Fig. IV-3.2 for hemming instructions).

Fig. VI-6.3 and Fig. VI-6.4 illustrate how your tunic can be gathered on one or both sides for interest. Stitch loosely two rows on the wrong side, pull the end threads to gather, and then permanently top-stitch two rows on the right side (Fig. VI-6.5). Optional: permanently top-stitch one or two rows on the right side using elasticized sewing thread.

(b) Make a Balloon Dress or Blouse from Dress Too Short

If you are the bold or the avant-garde type, you can easily convert a plain dress into an exotic balloon dress (Fig. VI-7.2) that is popular in European couture circles. Because the balloon dress is an evening garment, you should remove any sleeves and collar to keep the dress

simple so as not to detract from the skirt. To create Fig. VI-7.2,
loosely top-stitch close to the edge of the hem, gather as desired, and
then top-stitch to the edge of the hem some long, bold fringe in contrasting or complementary color. The length of the fringe should be
the length you want to add to your skirt. Repeat the color of the fringe
in a belt, jewelry, hose, or shoes. The balloon dress is great for
dinner dates and disco dancing; it would be more appropriately worn
on the American east coast than the west, and perfectly at home in Europe.

From a simple non-waisted dress you can easily make a blouson
top, always a classic (Fig. VI-7.3). Allow 2" (plus casing allowance)
from the waistline. Making the casing for the elastic is the same as
hemming a skirt (Fig. IV-3.2) except that the turn-up "hem" on the
wrong side of the blouson should be only 1/2" to 3/4" wide for the in-
sertion of the 1/4" to 3/8" wide elastic.

Fig. VI-7.4 illustrates a simple blouse (separate from the skirt)
which should be cut about 6" (plus hem allowance) from the waistline.
Optional for blouson dress: cut a blouson top 2" (plus casing allowance)
from the waistline. Keep the excess fabric from the dress too short to
make a new border skirt in another fabric in contrasting or complementary color or texture. Note that this new lengthening insert will have
to be cut to match up with the width of the blouson top (fully stretched
out) and the width of the border, which may have to be recut (see Fig.
V-6). Sew the very edge of the bottom of the blouson (fully stretched

out or without the elastic) to the top of the lengthening insert, right sides together. The elastic in the blouson casing will gather the skirt to fit your waistline. Wear with or without a belt.

(c) Make Skirts and Camisole from Dress Too Short

For a skirt from a non-waisted dress (Fig. VI-8.2), cut as shown in Fig. VI-8.1. Make a casing at the waist as shown in Fig. VI-8.4 and described for Fig. VI-7.3.

For the camisole (Fig. VI-8.3) make a casing at the top and bottom of the garment. The cutting guide lines on the dress in Fig. VI-8.1 are only suggested. If you want extra fullness in your camisole you may rather cut for it lower in the dress where you can get more material for extra fullness. The tennis skirt is a shorter version of the skirt in Fig. VI-8.2, although you may have to cut down the sides if you do not want too much fullness. Note that for either skirt you can use a draw string or narrow self belt through the casing. Make a buttonhole-like opening on the outside of the casing for passing through your ties.

(d) Miscellaneous Tops from Dress Too Short

Fig. VI-9 shows some additional tops you can make from the non-waisted dress (Fig. VI-9.1) not already mentioned in this chapter.

Fig. VI-9.2 is actually a blouson. Commercially-made knit ribbing was used for the waist and sleeve cuffs. With wrong sides together, stretch the ribbing taut to the fabric and top-stitch.

Variations of the knit-ribbed blouson include a hip-hugger length top,

long sleeves, and ribbed neckline. Also, you can use knit ribbing as

a waistband to make a short mini skirt (for active sports) to match

your top or mix with other tops for versatility.

Make a long, sleeveless bolero as shown in Fig. VI-9.3. Re-

move the sleeves and collar, if any, and cut down the center and across

at the hips. Hem edges as illustrated in Fig. IV-3.2, or face and hem

as shown in Fig. V-4.2.

Want a blouse like the one in Fig. VI-9.4? Just cut off the skirt

about 6" (plus hem allowance) below the waistline and hem. From the

excess skirt fabric, make a wide scarf (about 6") to tie around the neck

or the waist.

For a fun sun outfit as shown in Fig. VI-9.5, make a wide scarf

approximately 8" to 10" wide and long enough to wrap around your chest

in a tie. Use a commercial pattern to make the bandeau, or simply pull

the warp and weft threads to make the top. How to make the tennis skirt

is illustrated and described in Fig. VI-8.3.

The short-sleeved bolero in Fig. VI-9.6 is a short version of the

one in Fig. VI-9.3. Consider making a matching skirt, then adding long

fringe to both the hem of the skirt and the waist of the bolero. Team

the two pieces with a Western shirt and boots for a Western outfit. Or, wear the skirt and bolero with a red, bell-bottom sleeved blouse, high-heeled sandals, and gaucho hat for a Spanish look.

If you are the sporty, casual type, the midriff blouse in Fig. VI-9.7 is a top for you. Simply cut from 2" to 4" above the waist (plus hem allowance) and hem. The midriff may be cut coming to a point in front, or straight across, with long or short sleeves. Optional: work elastic through the hem (natural casing) for a fitted midriff.

(e) Let Out a Dress Too Tight

In addition to Fig. VI-5 on letting out a waisted dress too tight, Fig. VI-10 illustrates what you can do with the non-waisted dress too tight.

Fig. VI-10.1 shows how to rip open the side seams and trim the armhole area. Remove the sleeves, if any. The detailed insert shows how to face the seams and is further detailed in Fig. V-4.2.

Fig. VI-10.2 is one of the easiest methods of letting out a dress. For this style of dress you need not trim the armhole area. The grommets are available at yardage stores and come complete with instructions and installation tools. Use macramé thread for the lacings.

Fig. VI-10.3 is a simple tunic that can be worn belted or unbelted, with either skirts or pants or dresses.

Fig. VI-10.4 is only a variation of the former tunic, using the overcast stitch for decoration. Note that you could trim the edges of the tunic with grommets and overcast with the macramé lacings accordingly.

Fig. VI-1 - Make a Peplum Top from Dress Too Long or Too Short

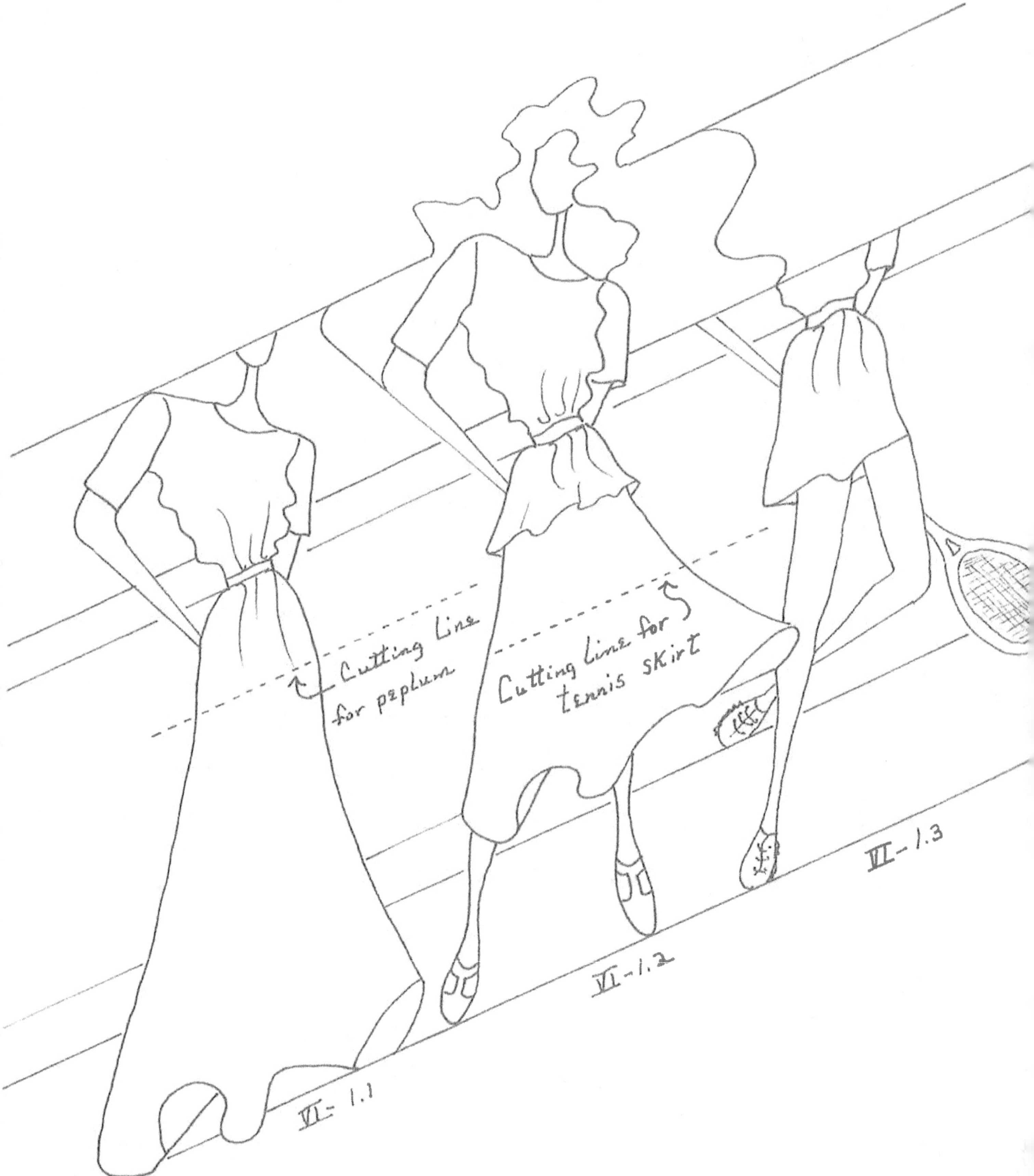

Cutting line for peplum

Cutting line for tennis skirt

VI-1.1

VI-1.2

VI-1.3

Fig. VI-a- Add a Tier or Border to Dress Too Short

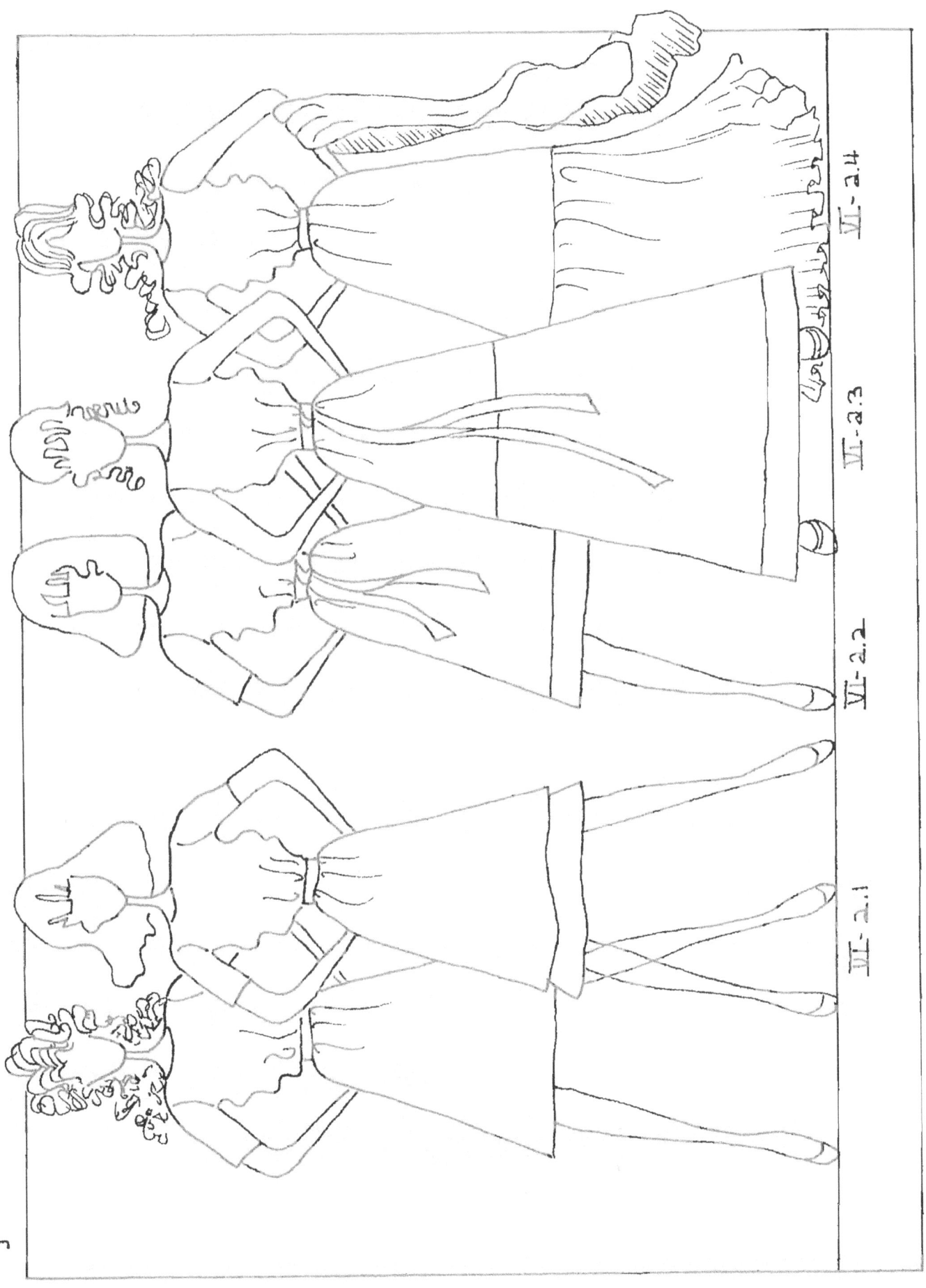

VI-2.1   VI-2.2   VI-2.3   VI-2.4

Fig. VI-3 - Make an Overskirt from Dress Too Long or Too Short

VI-3.4

VI-3.3

VI-3.1

VI-3.2

Cutting line for VI-3.4

Wrong Side

Fold line

Button hole

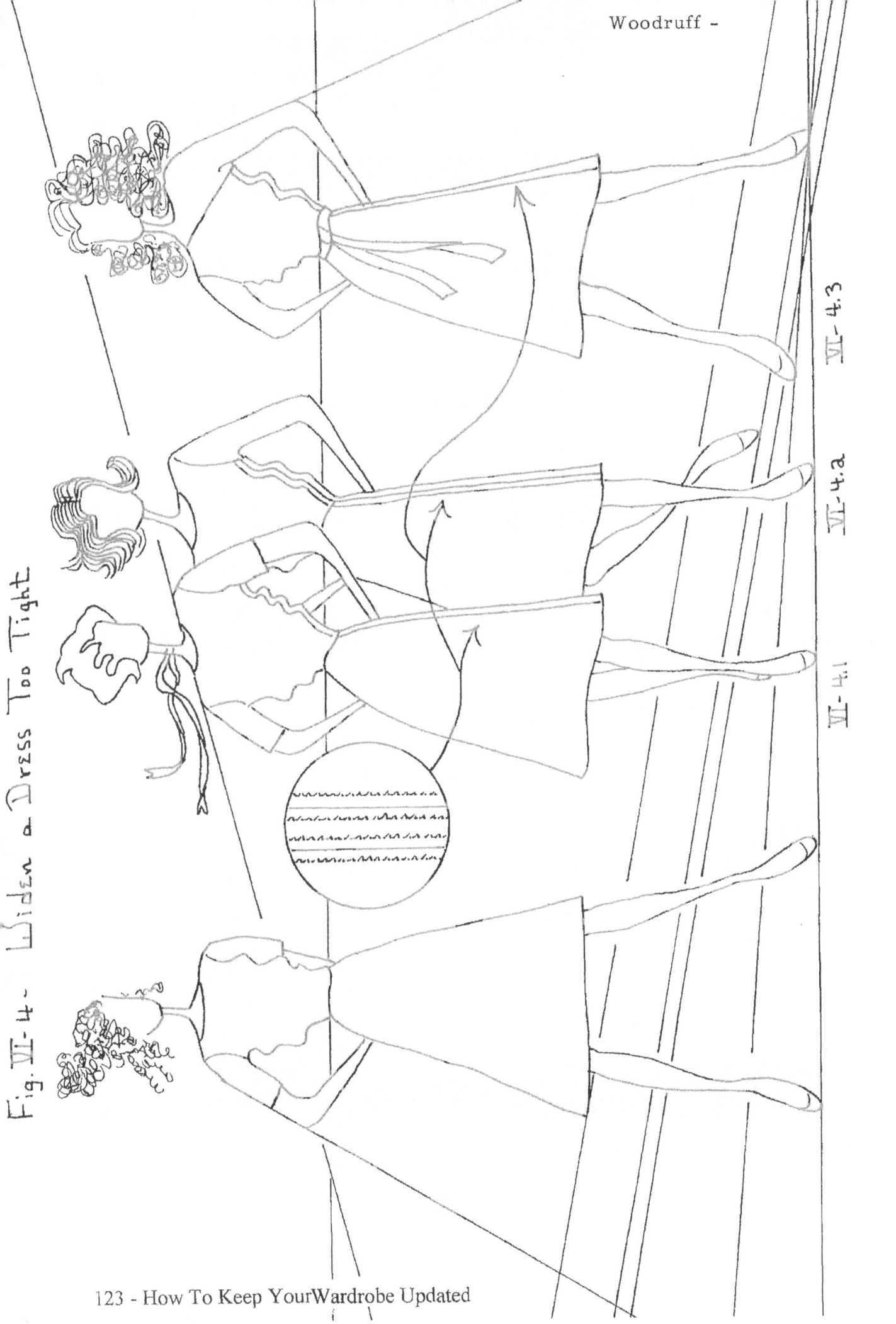

Fig.VI-4- Widen a Dress Too Tight

VI-4.3 VI-4.2 VI-4.1

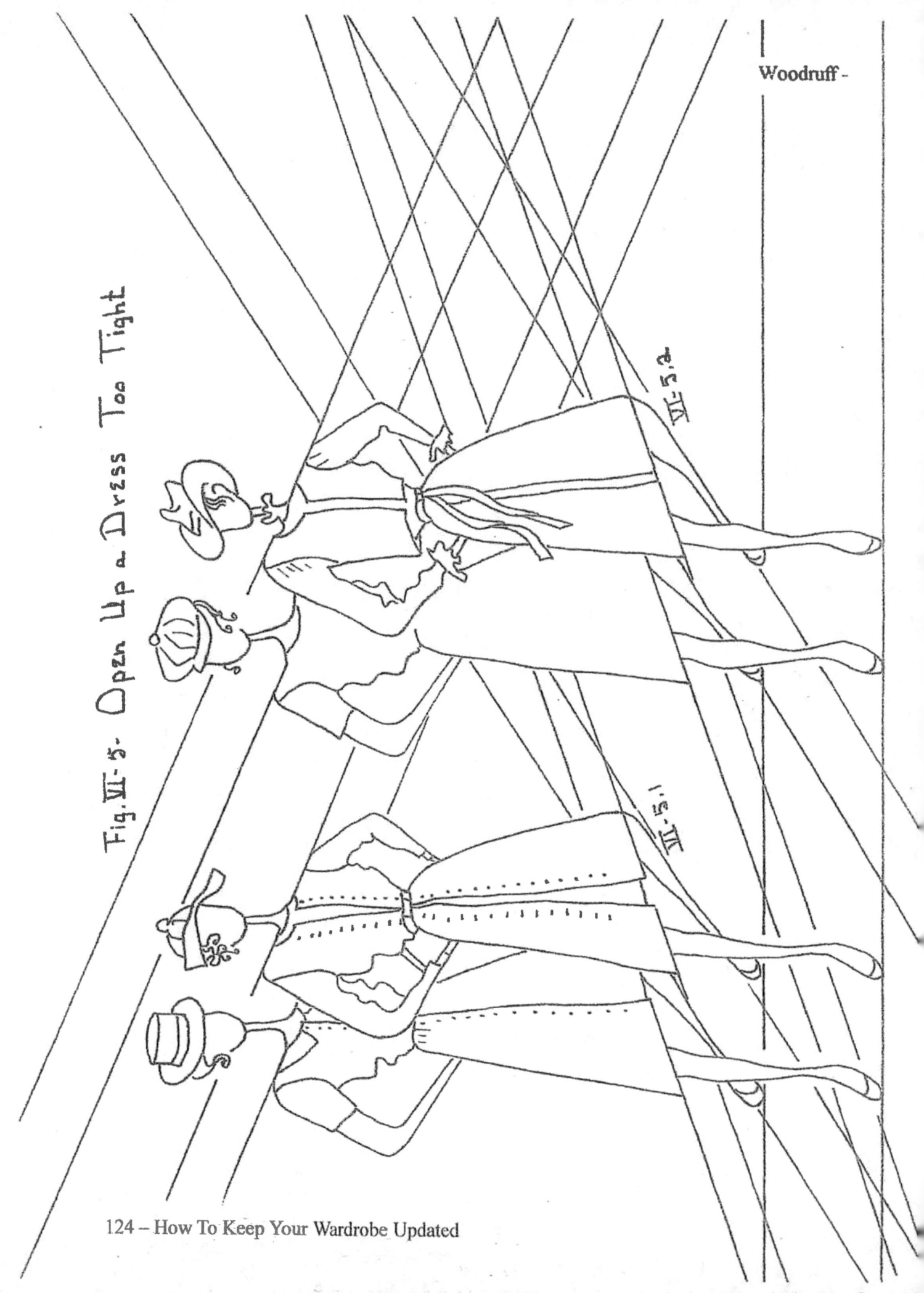

Fig. VI-5- Open Up a Dress Too Tight

VI-5.1

VI-5.3

Fig. VI-6 - Make a Tunic Top from Dress Too Short

Cut and hem for tunic

VI-6.1   VI-6.2   VI-6.3   VI-6.4   VI-6.5

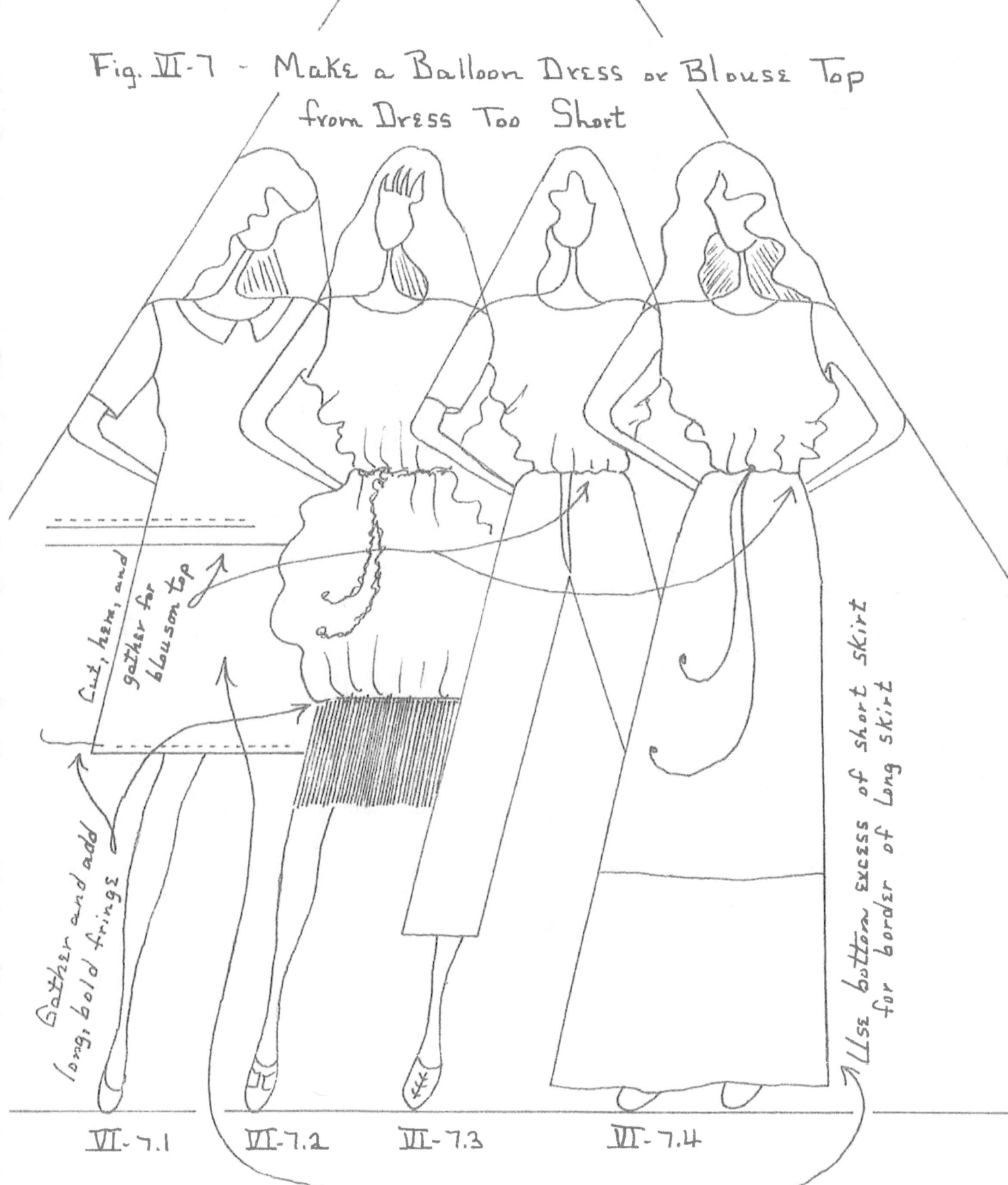

Fig. VI-7 - Make a Balloon Dress or Blouse Top from Dress Too Short

Cut, hem, and gather for blouson top

Gather and add long, bold fringe

Use bottom excess of short skirt for border of Long skirt

VI-7.1   VI-7.2   VI-7.3   VI-7.4

Fig. VI-8- Make Skirts and Camisole from Dress Too Short

elastic inside casing

VI-8.4

VI-8.1

VI-8.2

VI-8.3

Fig. VI-9 - Miscellaneous Tops from Dress Too Short

VI-9.2

VI-9.3

VI-9.1

VI-9.7

VI-9.6

VI-9.4

VI-9.5

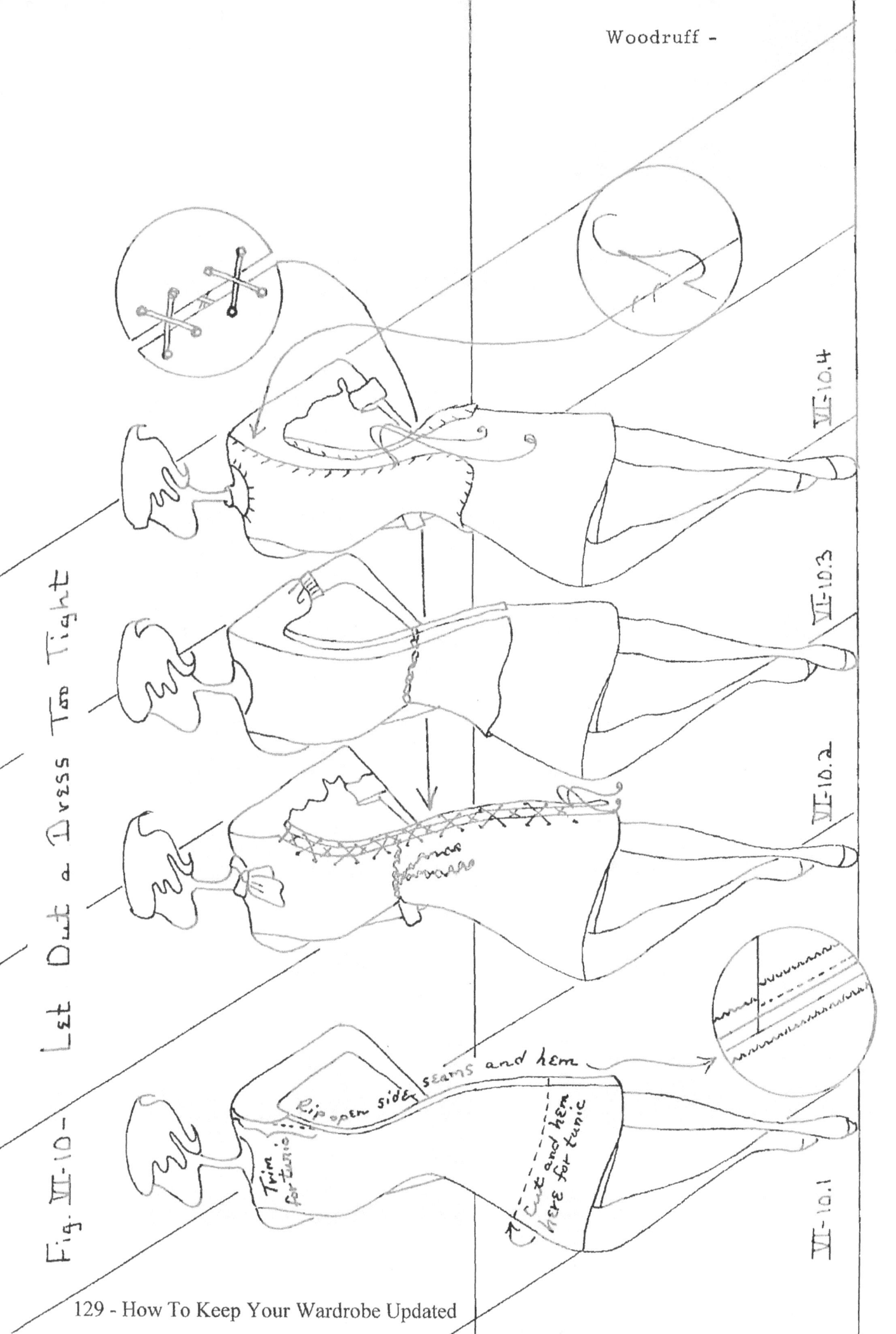

Fig. VI-10- Let Out a Dress Too Tight

VI-10.4

VI-10.3

VI-10.2

Rip open side seams and hem

Trim for tunic

Cut and hem here for tunic

VI-10.1

Chapter VII

Tops

Although this chapter deals specifically with all the different kinds of tops, it is really an extension of the previous chapter on dresses. For example, you may encounter the same collar and sleeve problems with your blouse as you would with your dress. I consider this chapter particularly important to keeping your wardrobe upgraded because tops add a great deal of diversity to your wardrobe, as discussed in detail in the first chapter.

1. Shirts Too Big

Although the models in the illustrations are wearing oversized men's shirts, this section also applies to the ladies' too big shirt blouse.

Fig. VII-1.1 illustrates how you can change the look of the blouse without altering the style. The sleeves are rolled up and the bodice bulk is taken in with a belt. The bulky, casual look is comfortable and fashionable for lounging at home, walking along the beach, or visiting in the country. Try wearing a pullover underneath the shirt for the layered look. If the shirt is much too big around the neck, wear the shirt open to the waist to expose a leotard suit for the gamin look. Or, wear the shirt with a black turtleneck, long-sleeved sweater, and black fishnet hose with high-heeled sandals for the glamorous city look. And remember that big, roomy clothes have become important in fashion among such great internationally-known designers as Norma Kamali, Giorgio Armani, and Sonia Rykiel.

The classic cossack shirt in Fig. VII-1.2 is an alternative to the big men's shirt. Remove the collar and the cuffs. Trim the collar stand, button placket, and shoulder seams with embroidered, tapestry-like trim. Use the same trim for a self-belt. Finally, cut the sleeves to desired length and hem them as you would hem a skirt (see Fig. IV-3.2). Then see Fig. IV-2.2 to make an elasticized hem casing from an existing hem. Wear the shirt with straight leg or cossack pants.

2. Cardigans Too Big

If your cardigan needs only slight alterations, simply take in the seams--see the guide lines in Fig. VII-2.1. Top-stitch twice (about twelve to fifteen stitches to the inch) before you cut any excess knit in order to prevent raveling. Note how the too big cuffs were merely tucked back and pinned with buttons (see Fig. VII-6.5 through Fig. VII-6.7 for detail).

For drastic alterations, refer to Fig. VII-2.3 and Fig. VII-2.4 on how you can redesign a cardigan. Draw your new sweater outline with chalk (Fig. VII-2.4) and be sure to allow for seam allowances. Top-stitch this outline twice (twelve to fifteen stitches to the inch) before you cut the sweater in order to prevent raveling. Use the same procedure for the sleeves. Finish the new cardigan with commercially-made knit ribbing, as shown in Fig. VII-2.3. This type of short sweater lends itself well to jewel-embroidered trim (commercially-made) around the neck, button and buttonhole plackets, waistline hem, and cuffs.

3. Pullovers Too Big

Pullovers that are too big can be treated exactly the same as the oversized cardigans illustrated in Fig. VII-2. Beyond that, the best thing you can do with the pullover that is too big or too loose is simply to belt it for the tunic look, as shown in Fig. VII-3.2. If the sleeves are too long, simply keep them pushed up over the elbow or roll them up.

An alternative to belting the pullover is to run a crotcheted string or macramé thread through the waist ribbing so that you can wear the sweater as a hip hugger blouson (Fig. VII-3.3). Note that paillettes (jumbo sequins) were used to give the pullover an expensive designer look. You can also use lightweight beads of varying sizes and colors to make yourself a one-of-a-kind artform. The paillettes and the beads can be removed before dry cleaning the garment in order to save cleaning expenses.

Fig. VII-3.4 is actually a version of Fig. VII-3.3 on a much lesser scale. Here the pullover hem and the sleeves were shortened and new knit ribbing was sewn at the waist and cuffs. This short sweater can also be converted to the blouson top by weaving a drawstring through the ribbed hem.

4. Sweater Tops Too Short or Too Tight

Fig. VII-4.1 and Fig. VII-4.4 illustrate what you can do with either the pullover or the cardigan too short or too tight.

For Fig. VII-4.2, refer to the Fig. VII-4.1 cutting guide lines (dotted lines). Use two rows of top-stitching (twelve to fifteen stitches to the inch) about 1/4" apart. Cut between these two rows in order to prevent raveling. Use knit inserts (or bands) in a contrasting or complementary color, as shown. Refer to Fig. V-5 for sewing instructions. Note that the stretch of the insert bands should give with the width of the body.

Fig. VII-4.3 is a midriff cut off from Fig. VII-4.1 with long fringe (or macramé and beads) attached to the hemline and the cuffs for the mod look. Again, be sure to make a row of top-stitching (twelve to fifteen stitches to the inch) before you cut the knit in order to prevent raveling.

To salvage a cardigan that is too tight (Fig. VII-4.4), rip off the sleeves and wear the garment unbuttoned as a bolero (Fig. VII-4.5). Use the sleeves to make leg warmers (Fig. VII-7.6).

An alternative to Fig. VII-4.5 is the sweater in Fig. VII-4.6. Rip open the underarm sleeve and bodice side seams and sew in side stripes in a contrasting or complementary color--the knit should stretch with the width of the body. This is the same concept that was used in Fig. IV-6.1.

5. Collar/Neckline Alterations

Frequently you can change the look of a garment by changing (or adding) the collar or the neckline. To illustrate the vast number of collar and neckline alterations and diversifications that are possible from most old, existing tops could fill a book and is beyond the scope of this work. Fig. VII-5 illustrates only a few ideas to serve as an impetus to help you start your own couture designs.

Commercially-made, detachable collars and dickeys are available in most styles. See Fig. VII-7.8 to make your own dickeys. Ties and scarves can do wonders to an otherwise plain neckline, as discussed in Chapter II. By means of layering, or wearing another garment under or over an existing garment, you can diversify the style of your necklines. For example, a short-sleeved top with a jewel neckline (Fig. VII-5.5) can be worn over a long-sleeved, turtleneck pullover

(Fig. VII-5.7). A basic polo shirt blouse (Fig. VII-5.3) can be worn unbuttoned over a turtleneck sweater (Fig. VII-5.7). Or a jewel (or crew) neckline (Fig. VII-5.5) pullover can be worn over a convertible shirt blouse (Fig. VII-5.2).

Let your imagination go and see how many diversifications you can create.

6.   Sleeve Alterations

(a) Sleeves Too Big or Too Long

The dotted lines in Fig. VII-6.1 are guide lines for reducing the size of the shoulder and sleeve areas. Most of the time this is the method you would probably choose to remedy sleeves that are too big or too long.

Fig. VII-6.2 through VII-6.7 are designer techniques that you can use to achieve the same end result for your sleeve alterations. For Fig. VII-6.2 refer to Fig. VI-3.5 for sewing instructions. For Fig. VII-6.3 to Fig. VII-6.7 refer to Fig. V-2.3. Consider using contrasting colored threads for the top-stitching for the designer look and repeat this color subtlely elsewhere: hair barrettes, stud earrings, a bracelet, hose. The pleats may be covered or coordinated with laces or trims and garnished with any decorative buttons or hardware.

(b) Sleeves Too Tight or Too Short

The easiest way to take care of sleeves too tight is to remove them and then cut down the underarm area of the bodice side seams, as shown in Fig. VII-6.8 and Fig. VII-6.9. With the deeper armpit (Fig. VII-6.9) you can wear your new sleeveless garment over other garments with sleeves.

Fig. VII-6.10 through Fig. VII-6.14 represent designer solutions to correct problem sleeves. Use a contrasting or complementary fabric, and cut the new sleeve pieces on straight grain of fabric, with the stretch, or give, running horizontally with the body. Repeat the new fabric elsewhere for the balanced look: self-belt, underskirt, head-band, scarf.

Fig. VII-6.11 represents the addition of an entirely new sleeve. Use the old sleeve as a guide to cutting out your new ones but be sure to add the extra allowance for the deepened armpit and/or sleeve length.

An alternative to the above are Fig. VII-6.12 and Fig. VII-6.13. Of the two methods, Fig. VII-6.12 is the easier: rip open the underarm sleeve and side bodice seams; cut an insert panel the desired width and length, plus seam and hem allowances--see Fig. IV-6.1 for sewing instructions. The insert in Fig. VII-6.13 is on the same principle as the previous illustration except that the top of the sleeve must be cut and the shoulder seam (of the bodice) must be trimmed to align with the new sleeve seams.

If you have a short sleeve that is too tight in the upper arm area only, insert a godet in the sleeve as shown. Refer to Fig. IV-6.3 for detailed sewing instructions.

7. Special Repairs for Knit Tops

There is nothing more discouraging than an otherwise good sweater ruined by perspiration stains, a rip, worn thin elbows, or sagging hemline. The good news is that even drastic damage to your sweater need not mean the end of the garment. Learn to recycle.

Fig. VII-7.1 illustrates a sweater with the underarm area badly damaged due to perspiration, a rip in the front of the bodice, and a worn out elbow. Most people would not hesitate to throw out such a top. However, as Fig. VII-7.2 shows, the entire sleeve was removed and the armpit area cut down. Face the armhole with grosgrain ribbon. Then top-stitch along the dotted lines just above the rip and the hemline (twelve to fifteen stitches to the inch), and resew the ribbed hem or sew on an entirely new one. And note that leg warmers (Fig. VII-7.6) can be made from the sleeves if the elbows are not damaged. See Fig. IV-2.2 for top and bottom natural casing. Wear the leg warmers with any of the altered tops shown in Fig. VII-7.

As an alternative, see the self-explanatory illustrations in Fig. VII-7.3 and Fig. VII-7.4 to repair the perspiration marks.

Apply commercially-made elbow patches (Fig. VII-7.5), often used decoratively on expensive sweaters and jackets, to the worn out elbow area.

The tank top in Fig. VII-7.7 is a version of the top in Fig. VII-7.2. The neck is cut down and a kangaroo front pocket is added (from the sleeves). Commercially-made knit ribbing was used to trim the neckline, armholes, and waistline for the coordinated look.

If the knit top is severely damaged, you might consider making a dickey (Fig. VII-7.8). Remember to outline the edge with a row of top-stitching (twelve to fifteen stitches to the inch) before cutting to prevent raveling.

Another possibility for a seemingly damaged-beyond-salvaging knit top is the camisole in Fig. VII-7.9. See Fig. IV-2.2 to make a natural casing for the top and bottom of the camisole, or sew on commercially-made knit ribbing to fit your body.

8. Special Upgrading Techniques

(a) Craftsworks

Almost any craft, in any myriad of media, can be incorporated into your piece of clothing to give it renewed interest. These include: crewel embroidery, fabric painting, macramé, leather patchwork, crotcheting, grommeting, patchwork quilting, and beadwork, just to name a few. As examples for you to create your own designs, try: crewel embroidery decorating an old wool cardigan (Fig. VII-8.1); fabric painting gracing a favorite sweat shirt (Fig. VII-8.2); macramé circling the hem of a top (Fig. VII-8.3); leather patchwork covering a Western vest (Fig. VII-8.4); crotchet squares (say 3"x3") complementing a plain pullover (Fig. VII-8.5); grommets peak-a-booing through a leather top (Fig. VII-8.6); patchwork squares quilting shirt pockets (Fig. VII-8.7); beadwork outlining one print in a pattern of a blouse (Fig. VII-8.8).

(b) Buttons

Often a little goes a long way. Good quality buttons are an instant upgrader. A good cotton blouse will look more expensive with real brass buttons, for example (Fig. VII-8.9). Or try using decorative buttons, like red hearts, for example, then repeat the red hearts in embroidery (satin stitch) scattered on the cuffs and/or sleeves for the couture look (Fig. VII-8.10). Or drape a silk scarf around the neck, if the top is collarless, cover the buttons with one end of the scarf, and button through the buttonholes with some of the scarf showing beyong the edge of the placket (Fig. VII-8.11).

(c) Special Collage Works

Do you have an old jacket or cardigan you want to throw out? Don't. Collage it. If you collect campaign buttons or sports badges, for example, use your garment as a display for your collection (Fig. VII-8.12 and Fig. VII-8.13 respectively). Many islanders and primitive cultures make beautiful embroidery works and embellishments on small cotton squares, say 12"x12", that you can use to cover the back of your own jacket or cardigan and end up with an exotic, one-of-a-kind, ethnic garment (Fig. VII-8.14). Or, use scraps of laces and trims as your collage work (Fig. VII-8.15). And that little wool cardigan will take on new importance with leather buttons (see Buttons, this chapter) and leather patches (Fig. VII-8.16), available commercially-made.

(d) Top-Stitching and Outlining

Hand top-stitching is a work of fine quality and workmanship. Use top-stitching in contrasting thread (running stitch) to perk up a tired bolero (Fig. VII-8.17), or boost an otherwise plain white shirt blouse-- use a running stitch to outline the armholes of the bodice, the shoulder seams, and bodice sides (Fig. VII-8.18). Or trim your Chanel cardigan with leather lacings in an overlap stitch (Fig. VII-8.19); or try outlining the Chanel cardigan with metal beads (Fig. VII-8.20)--beads and installation instructions are available in kits at yardage stores.

(e) Special Trims

Special trims are discussed briefly in Fig. V-9 for skirts; the same ideas can be applied to tops. Consider such possibilities as fringe outlining an old poncho (Fig. VII-8.21) which can dual as a skirt (really); lace trim adorning a shirt placket (Fig. VII-8.22); decorative appliques embellishing a dinner jacket (Fig. VII-8.23); ruffles dancing down the sleeves of a plain blouse (Fig. VII-8.24); a decorative, contrasting zipper zipping down one sleeve of a sporty blouse. All trims mentioned are available commercially-made at yardage stores.

*** *** ***

These ideas should serve only as an impetus for you to design your own couture creations. Only a skeletal sketch of upgrading techniques is presented here. Virtually unlimited possibilities are feasible but beyond the scope of mention in this work. I hope that the few samples suggested here will serve as a springboard for you to create your own boutique collection. Many ideas in this chapter may be extended to upgrading skirts, pants, and dresses. Pick something simple, such as modern fabric painting, practice your design on paper first, then pin the mock up design on to your garment before making your transfer. Depending on your crafts talents, there are boundless possibilities for you to explore, as well as to gain interest in pursuing new craft arts that can become a part of your beautiful, one-of-a-kind couture designs. Public libraries are replete with hobby and craft how-to books in every field of crafts art. Also explore magazines for ideas.

Fig. VII-1 - Shirts Too Big

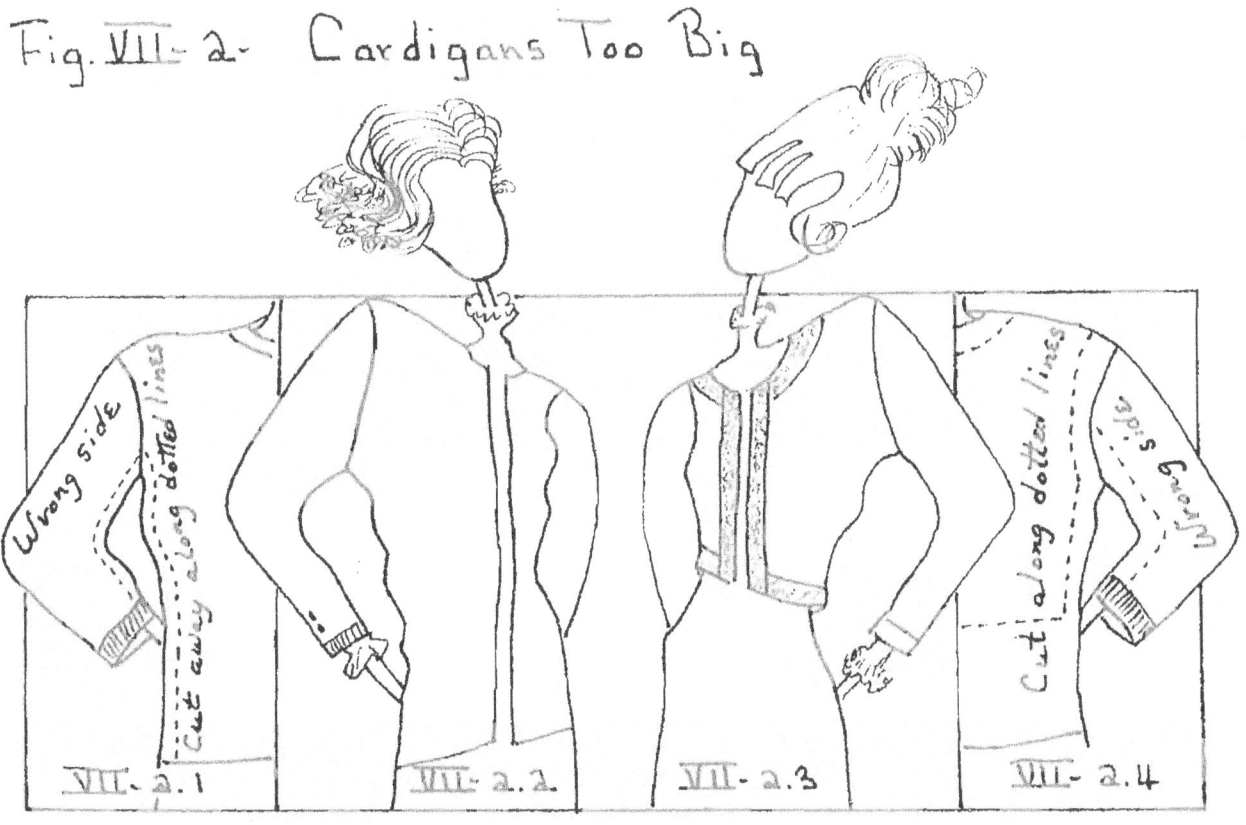

shoulder seam

collar stand

button placket

VII-1.1

VII-1.2

See Fig. IV-2.2 to make elasticized hem casing

Fig. VII-2- Cardigans Too Big

Wrong side

Cut away along dotted lines

Cut along dotted lines

Wrong side

VII-2.1

VII-2.2

VII-2.3

VII-2.4

Fig. VII-3 - Pullovers Too Big

VII-3.1 VII-3.2 VII-3.3 VII-3.4

Fig. VII-4- Sweater Tops Too Short or Too Tight

Fig. VII-5- Collar/Neckline Alterations

Basic Convertible

Cutting guide for smaller collar

VII-5.1

Remove collar for mandarin collar

VII-5.2

Wear open for polo shirt look

VII-5.3

Basic Peter-Pan Collar

Remove collar for Fig. 5.5, 5.6 and 5.7

Cutting guide for

VII-5.4

Jewel Neckline

VII-5.5

"V-neckline"

VII-5.6

Off One Shoulder

VII-5.8

VII-5.7

Mock Turtle Neck

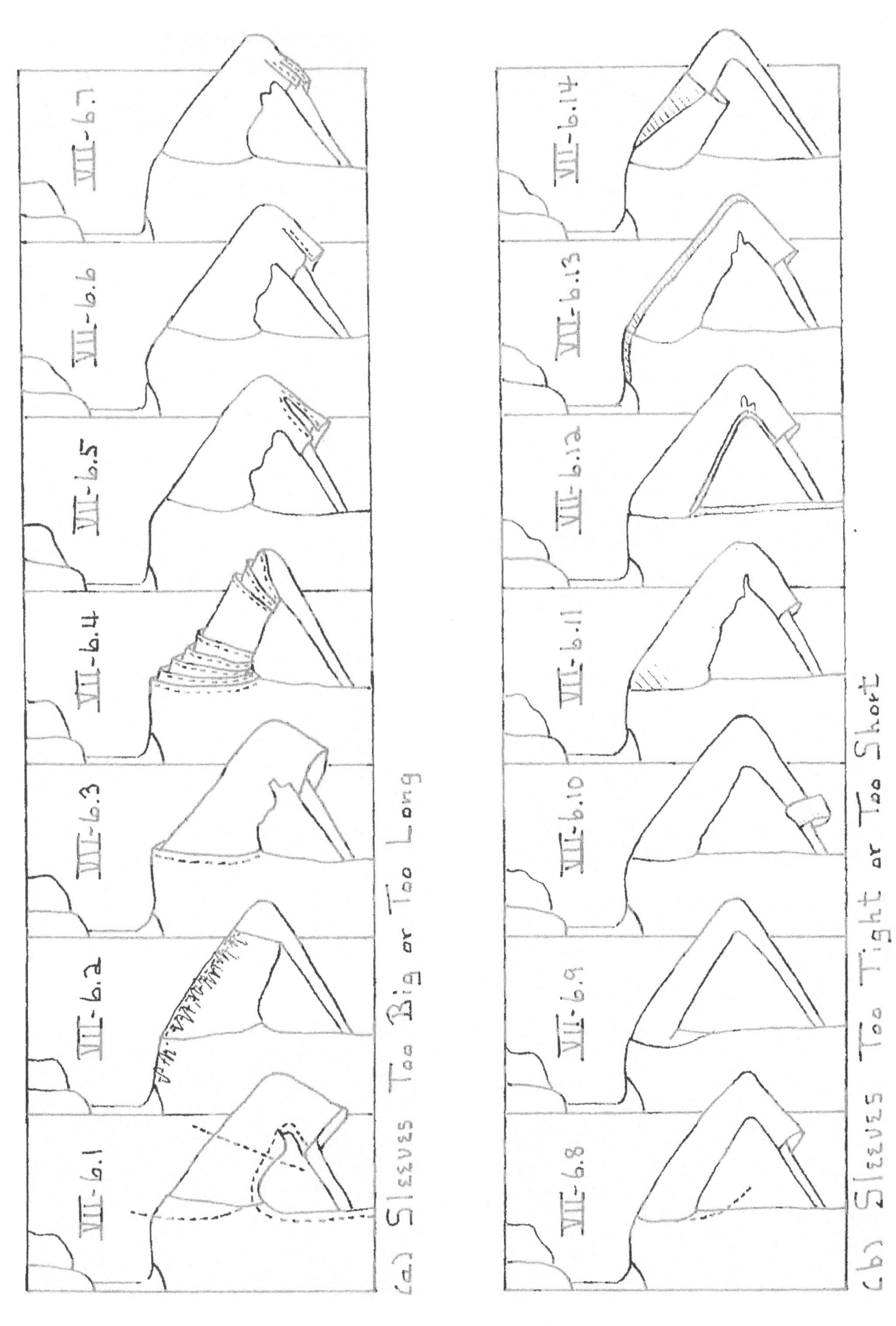

Fig. VII-6 - Sleeve Alterations

(a) Sleeves Too Big or Too Long

VII-6.1   VII-6.2   VII-6.3   VII-6.4   VII-6.5   VII-6.6   VII-6.7

(b) Sleeves Too Tight or Too Short

VII-6.8   VII-6.9   VII-6.10   VII-6.11   VII-6.12   VII-6.13   VII-6.14

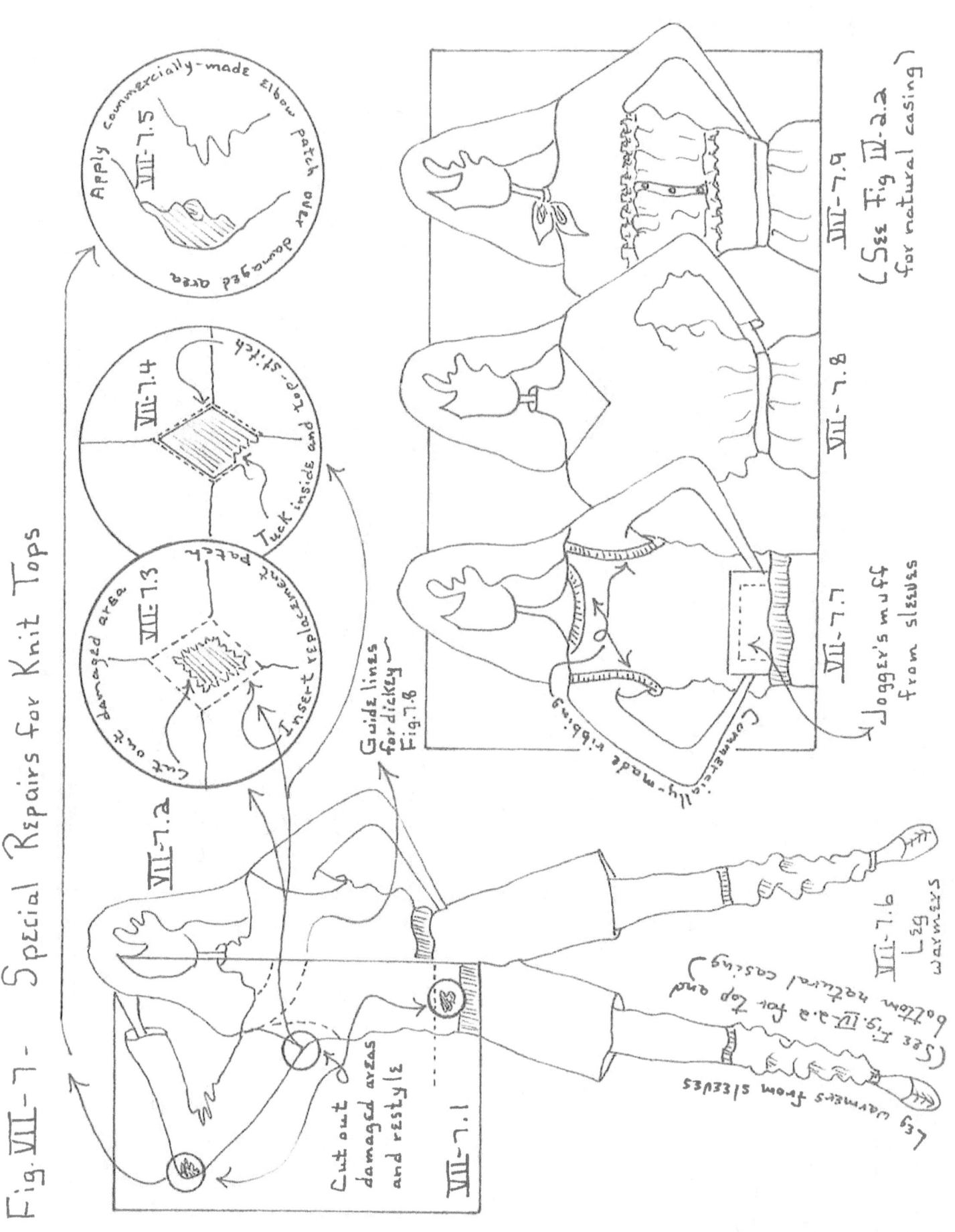

Fig. VII-7- Special Repairs for Knit Tops

VII-7.5 — Apply commercially-made elbow patch over damaged area

VII-7.4 — Tuck inside and top-stitch

VII-7.3 — Cut out damaged area — Insert replacement patch

VII-7.2

Guide lines for dickey Fig. 7.8

Cut out damaged areas and restyle

VII-7.1

VII-7.9 — (See Fig. III-3.3.a for natural casing)

VII-7.8

VII-7.7 — Jogger's muff from sleeves

Commercially-made ribbing

VII-7.6 — Leg warmers

(See Fig. III-3.3.a for top and bottom natural casing)

Leg warmers from sleeves

Fig. VII-8. Special Upgrading Techniques
(A Supplement to Fig. IV-4 and Fig. V-9)

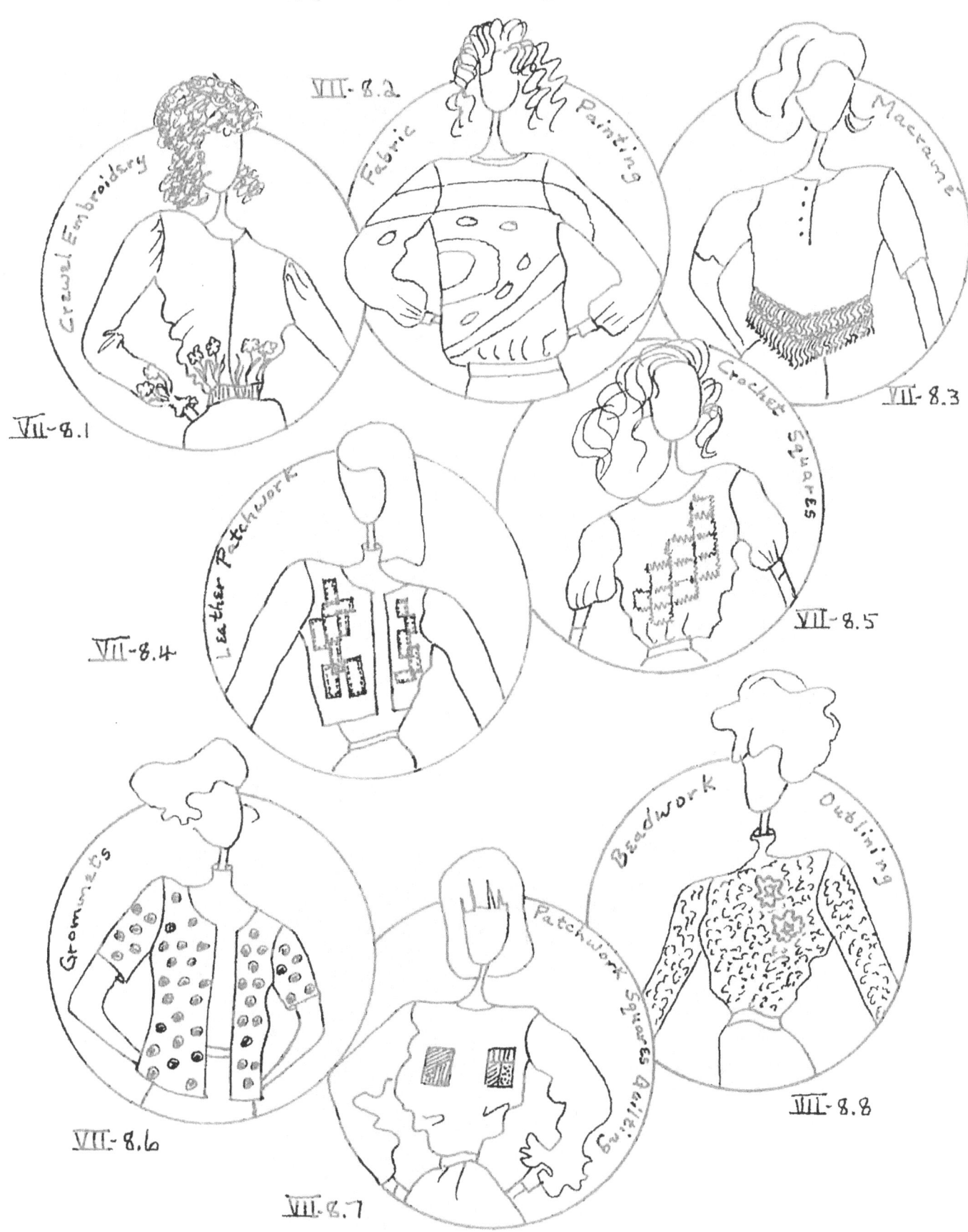

VII-8.2

Crewel Embroidery

VII-8.1

Fabric Painting

Macrame

VII-8.3

Leather Patchwork

VII-8.4

Crochet Squares

VII-8.5

Grommets

VII-8.6

Patchwork Squares Quilting

VII-8.7

Beadwork

Outlining

VII-8.8

(a) Craftsworks

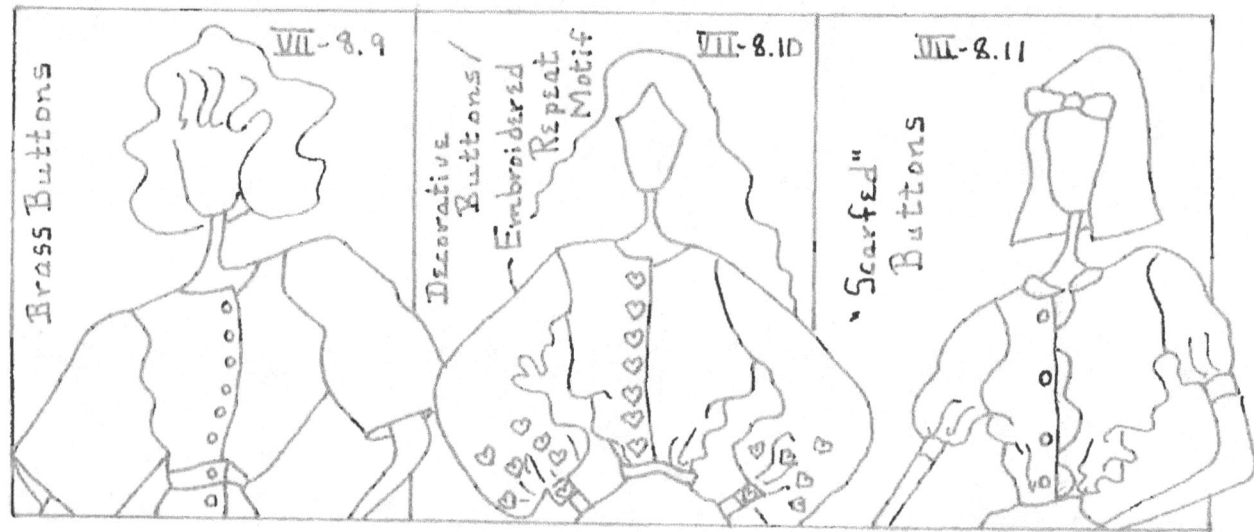

Brass Buttons   VII-8.9

Decorative Buttons/ Embroidered Repeat Motif   VII-8.10

"Scarfed" Buttons   VII-8.11

(b) Buttons

Button Display   VII-8.12

Sports Badges   VII-8.13

"Primitive" Soft Art   VII-8.14

Laces and Trims Collage   VII-8.15

Leather Patches   VII-8.16

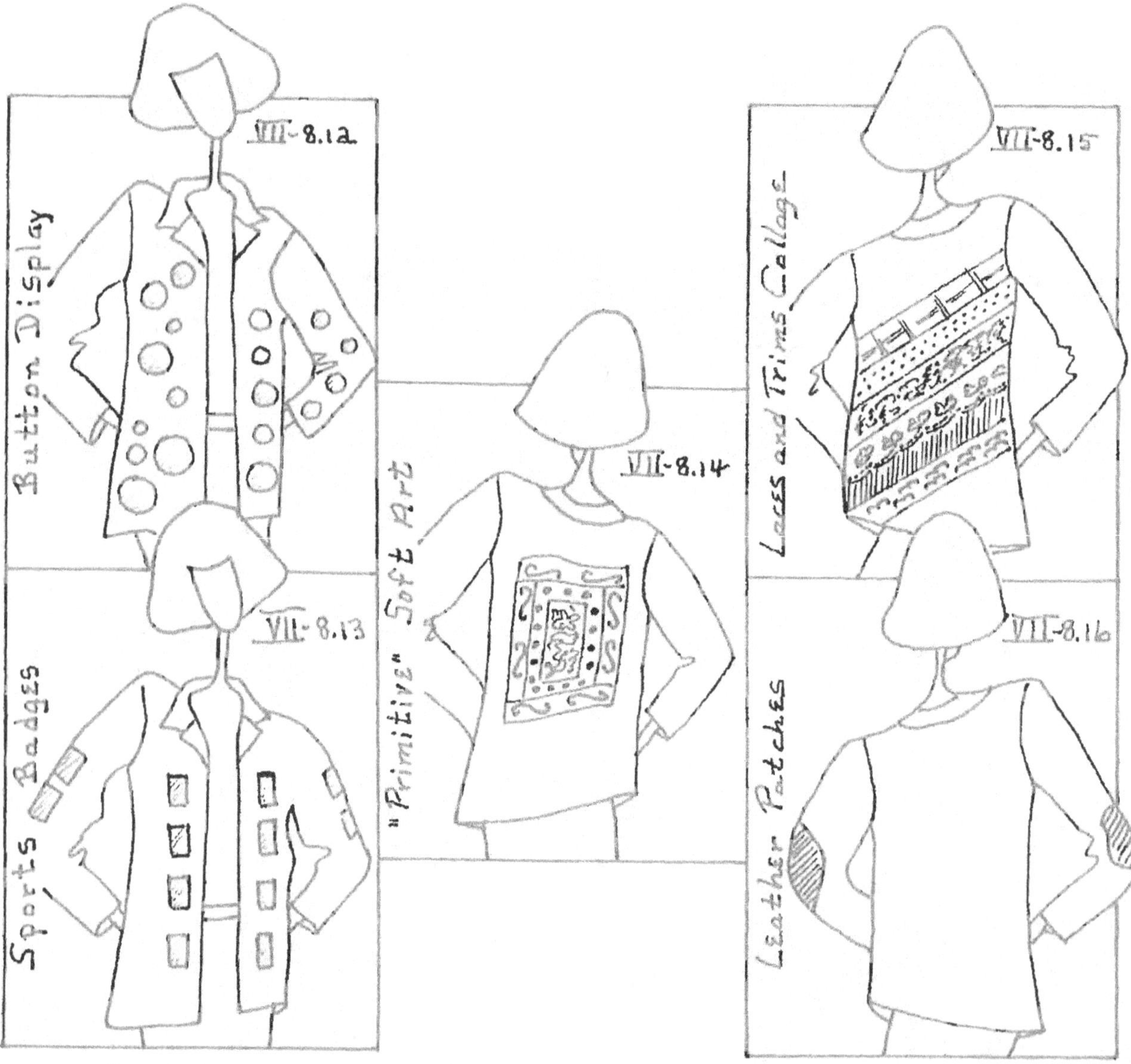

(c) Special Collage Works

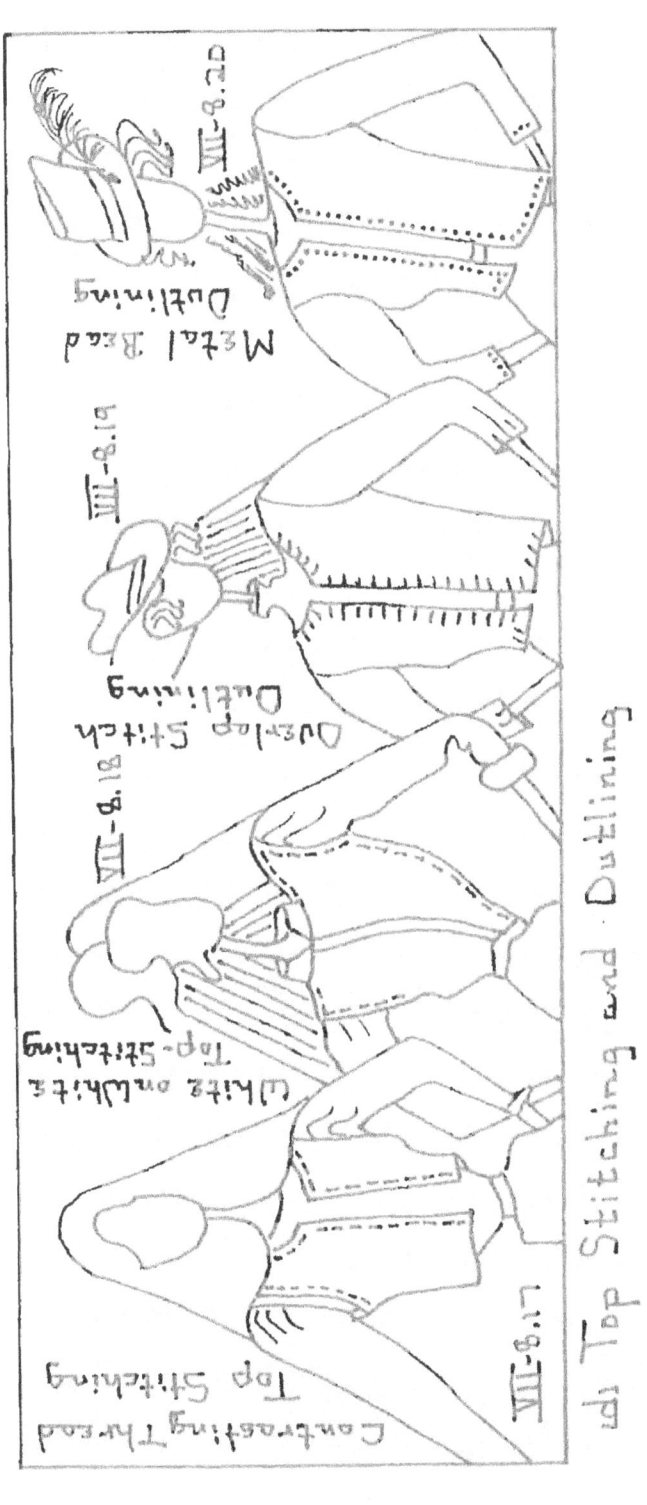

VII-8.20
Metal Bead
Outlining

VII-8.19
Overlap Stitch
Outlining

VII-8.18
White on White
Top-Stitching

VII-8.17
Contrasting Thread
Top Stitching

(d) Top Stitching and Outlining

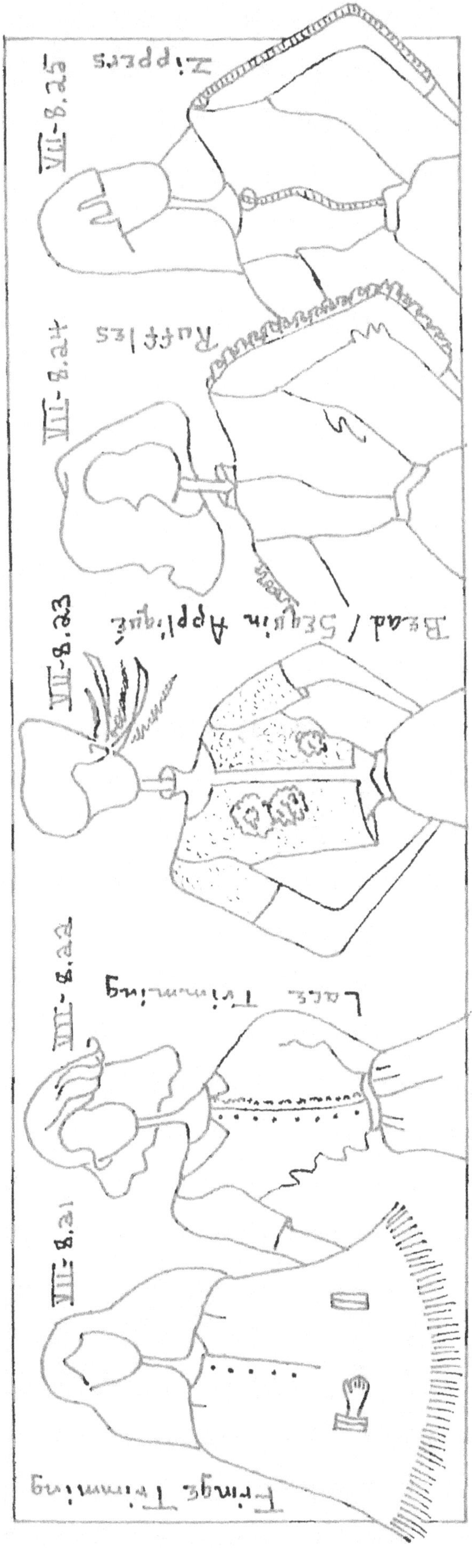

VII-8.25
Zippers

VII-8.24
Ruffles

VII-8.23
Bead / Sequin Appliqué

VII-8.22
Lace Trimming

VII-8.21
Fringe Trimming

(e) Special Trims (commercially-made)

Chapter VIII

Jackets and Related Outer Garments

Jackets and outer garments can be redesigned and upgraded in the same manner as any other items of clothing. Use the same techniques to alter and upgrade your jackets and other outer garments as you would skirts, dresses, and tops, discussed in Chapters V, VI, and VII.

1.   Jackets and Outer Garments Too Long or Too Short

For jackets and coats too long, simply cut and hem up as you would your skirts--see Chapter V, Fig. V-2 and Fig. V-3. For jackets and coats too short, refer to Chapter V, Fig. V-4 through Fig. V-9.

2.   Jackets and Outer Garments Too Big or Too Tight

To alter jackets and coats too big, refer to Chapter VII, Fig. VII-2, Fig. VII-3, Fig. VII-4, and Fig. VII-6. To alter jackets and coats too tight, refer to Chapter VI, Fig. VI-5 and Fig. VI-10, and Chapter VII, Fig. VII-4 and Fig. VII-6.

3.   Special Problems for Jackets and Outer Garments

For any special problems you may have with your jackets and coats, refer to Chapter VII, Fig. VII-4, Fig. VII-5, and Fig. VII-6.

4. <u>Special Repairs for Jackets and Outer Garments</u>

For any special repairs for jackets and coats, refer to Chapter VII, Fig. VII-7.

5. <u>Special Upgrading Techniques for Jackets and Outer Garments</u>

For any special upgrading techniques for jackets and coats, refer to Chapter IV, Fig. IV-4, Chapter V, Fig. V-9, and Chapter VII, Fig. VII-8.

Chapter IX

Miscellaneous Accessories Upgrading Techniques

1. Footwear

Leather footwear improves with age; therefore, with minimal maintenance, you can considerably extend the life of your footwear. Apart from the obvious polishing of your footwear to keep it upgraded, consider recycling. If the leather heels are beyond repair, reheel-- wood stack heels for day shoes; glass heels for evening shoes. Shoes worn through? Resole. Threads ripped? Repair professionally. Tired of the color? Redye professionally. Tired of those poi de soi slippers? Add rhinestone buckles or a contrasting bow (that matches something in your ensemble). Oxford shoes need a pickup? Consider some spiffy laces. All of these renovations will make your shoes look like new at a fraction of the cost of new footwear.

2. Handbags

Like footwear, a good cleaning (with saddle soap and warm water) and polishing can work wonders to upgrade your handbag. And good leather improves with age here too. Shoulder strap or handle beyond repair? Replace it with a handbag chain (from your dog's old leash). Need a splash of color? Drape a silk scarf from one side of your handbag. For a cloth handbag, add a bright pin. Unless you are a master in leatherworks, most of the upgrading should be handled by professional leather craftspeople (or shoe repair people). Metal

trimmings dull? Stitching ripped? Tooling torn? Have the work done

professionally to give your handbag a new look at a fraction of the cost

of a new handbag. Do you have a fabric evening handbag that needs

upgrading? Have it drycleaned professionally. Consider bead appliques

(commercially made) to attach to your handbag. Handle or shoulder

strap frazzled? Replace it with light weight metal chain or silk cord.

3.   Belts

Apart from keeping your leather belts well polished, any upgrading--

stitching, metal replacing--should be done by professional craftspeople.

Refer to the above two chapters on Footwear and Handbags for upgrading

belts. Most belts will probably be made of fabric to match or contrast

with your outfits, in which case the belt will be drycleaned or laundered.

Fabric belts can always be decorated with scarves, jewelry, embroidery,

grommets and lacings, laces and trims, even furs and feathers. See

also Chapter II on Belts.

APPENDIX I

Types of Wool

albatross	cashmere	harris tweed	sealskin
albert cloth	cavalry twill	homespun	serge
alpaca	challis	Irish tweed	sharkskin
Andalusians	cheviot	Jacob tweed	shepherd check
angora	chinchilla	jersey	shetland
armure	corkscrew cloth	kersey	tartan
astrakhan	covert cloth	Lincoln green	tattersall
baize	crossbred	loden	tropical cloths
bannockburn	delaine	Mackinaw cloth	tweed
barathea	doeskin	melton	vicuna
beaver cloth	duffel	mohair	viyella
bedford cord	elastique	moquette	whipcord
billiard cloth	etamine	Navajo blanket	zibeline (or ripple cloth)
blanket	felt	nun's veiling	
blazer cloth	flannel	paisley	
botany	fleece fabrics	pattu	
broadcloth	frieze	piano cloth	
buckskin	frisé	plaid	
bunting	gabardine	plush	
cadet cloth	glen checks	ratiné	
camel hair	haircloth	saxony	

APPENDIX II

Types of Silk

aerophane	mashru	tussah
atlas	mienchow	velvet
bengaline de soie	milanese	
bolting cloth	moiré	
bourette	mousseline de soie	
brocade	ninon	
brocatelle	ottoman	
broché	panne velvet	
chiffon	parachute silk	
corah silk	pongee	
crêpe de chine	poult	
damask	radium	
duchesse satin	radzimir	
epingle	satin	
faille	shantung	
foulard	shot silk	
grosgrain	surah	
georgette	taffeta	
habutai	thai silk	
morocain	tricot	
marquisette	tulle	

APPENDIX III

Types of Cotton

airplane cloth	chambray	jean	piqué
atlas	cheesecloth	kain	plissé
awning cloth	chino	kanga (khanga)	poplin
balbriggan	chintz	khadi (khaddar)	sateen
balloon fabric	cleaning cloths	khaki	seersucker
bandanna	clydella	kitenge (kitangi)	sponge cloth
basket cloth	corduroy	lawn	stockinette
batiste	cretonne	long cloth	surgical cloths
bird's eye	denim	madras	tarlatan
book cloth	dimity	matelassé	toweling
broadcloth	dotted swiss	moleskin	ticking
broderie anglaise	drill	monk's cloth	velour
buckram	duck	mull	velveteen
bump cloth	dungaree	muslin	venetian cloth
calico	duvetine	nainsook	voile
candlewick	flannelette	oil cloth	winceyette
canton flannel	fustian	oilskin	
cantoon	gauze	organdie	
canvas	gingham	osnaburg	
casement	jaconet	oxford cloth	
cellular	jasper cloth	percale	

www.ingramcontent.com/pod-product-compliance
Lightning Source LLC
Chambersburg PA
CBHW081826280526
45789CB00007B/2353